IN PRAISE OF GENTLEMEN

In Praise of GENTLEMEN

BY

HENRY DWIGHT SEDGWICK

Nicht Stimmenmehrheit ist des Rechtes Probe
— SCHILLER

Essay Index Reprint Series

BOOKS FOR LIBRARIES PRESS
FREEPORT, NEW YORK

First Published 1935
Reprinted 1970

STANDARD BOOK NUMBER:
8369-1536-4

LIBRARY OF CONGRESS CATALOG CARD NUMBER:
74-107737

PRINTED IN THE UNITED STATES OF AMERICA

Hic Libellus
H. P. S. *et* A. de F. S.
Nuribus Jucundissimis
Grato Animo Dedicatus Est

INTRODUCTION

IT is over a hundred years since the last of the *Waverley Novels* was written, and the mere name of those famous books, which swept down from Edinburgh over England, France, Germany, and Italy, and stirred their generation to wild enthusiasm, helps us to realize the revolution that has metamorphosed social ideas and usages since then. Some of these novels still maintain a foremost place in English literature, and yet the present generation holds them cheap; it reads *Rob Roy* and *The Heart of Midlothian,* if at all, as monuments in literary history. And this is due less to a change in literary taste than to the revolution in social usages and ideas. The young generation derides Scott's admiration for high rank in the social hierarchy as snobbery, it calls his loyalties prejudices, it denounces his moral delicacy as puritanical prudery; it measures them by its own standards, its own usages, its own ideas, and finds them wanting. It would be idle to speculate whether their standards or those of Sir Walter are more conducive to general happiness. In any

INTRODUCTION

event, the change is historically interesting and has its place in the story of civilization.

In Scott's day there was a sentiment of humility abroad and men gladly accepted something higher than themselves, natural or supernatural, to admire, to reverence, or to worship, and Sir Walter greatly enjoyed this spirit of humility. His sympathies spread wide from kings and cavaliers to outlaws, smugglers, and gypsies; the drama of life exhilarated him, but his feeling of admiration gave him the most abiding pleasure. He rejoiced to look up to superior men, but only when his generous charity could attribute to them the qualities which, as he conceived, enter into the making of a gentleman. I am not concerned, of course, with his ill success in giving life to his heroes, — inartistic congeries of gentlemanly qualities, — but merely with his conception of what those qualities should be. By the term "gentleman" he meant a man born with social advantages, who lived true to his creed — to be brave, and, as far as his physical nature permitted, strong and skillful in bodily exercises, truthful, loyal, modest, romantically devoted to one woman, cultivated without pedantry, joyful in the good things of life, magnanimous, generous, not indifferent to dress, and very solicitous for courtesy.

I do not say that Scott was right in his notions,

[viii]

nor do I say that any one of these ingredients in his conception of a gentleman has wholly lost all value in the eyes of the present generation; but the conception of these ingredients in combination, as Scott combined them in his ideal gentleman, is sinking fast behind our new social horizon. Even fifty years ago, according to report, a distinguished professor at Harvard University said to his class, "Probably none of you young men have ever seen a gentleman." And now even the ideal is gone, like an old fashion in dress, not spoken of but to be laughed at. Is this gain or loss? This question I shall examine in the ensuing chapters.

CONTENTS

[xi]

CONTENTS

PART THREE

The forces of destruction

PART ONE

*On the qualities necessary to membership in
the Guild of Gentlemen*

I

THE GENTLEMAN DEFINED

OLD people, gloomy people, moralizing people, and some others besides, say that our times are out of joint. And so, to the contemplative mind, they often seem. A great change has come over ideas concerning life and its values; a revolution has taken place in our sentiments, manners, and moral opinions; and this, as Edmund Burke says, is "the most important of all revolutions." Every past generation has differed in one respect or another from that preceding it, for life consists in changes; but the present generation is exorbitantly different from that before the Great War. Some think that the War wrought this transformation, but the War merely helped and hastened this break in continuity, for the old order had long been growing fragile and tenuous, and would have given way, though less abruptly, to the new order (if such a term may be applied to our present social condition) through the working of various destructive forces. However, the sum

[3]

of changes that has taken and is taking place in our conceptions of civilization lies quite beyond my present purpose, which is the modest task of considering but one element in this change, and that is the reversal of the time-honored notion that the qualities which make a gentleman are qualities valuable to society; that a gentleman is part of the social, moral, and spiritual wealth of a people, and deserves esteem equally with persons of economic or other utilitarian worth.

Throughout the course of European history, the group of men whom we call gentlemen, distinguished from their fellows by inward qualities as well as by various exterior characteristics, has been produced and sustained by a general belief that society at large gained and gained greatly by the establishment and maintenance of an element within itself that should serve as guide and mentor to the general mass of men, blinded and confused as they are in the hugger-mugger of workaday life. This group did not constitute a class, but rather a body that in divers ways resembled a club or a guild. I shall refer to it as the Guild of Gentlemen. Its characteristics changed with the changing needs, experiences, and tastes of successive generations; but it always possessed, to a greater or less degree, sufficient continuity, sufficient adherence to tradition, to principles, for its members to be readily recognized as belonging to the Guild. The outward marks consisted in the main of manners, a habit of carriage, of gesture, a modulation of the voice, a regard for dress — as, for example, with Pericles, who always observed a "decency of dress such that no vehemence of speaking ever put in disorder." This care of personal appearance was partly a manifestation of self-respect, the moral equivalent of heraldic blazonry, but most of all it was due to the purpose of expressing the qualities within — urbanity, tact, measure, as in certain types of architecture it is held that the façade should be an exponent of the structure behind. And more than that, outward appearance sought to reveal the self, not as it is, but rather as it should be, or as it is at its best — solicitous for elegance, for the niceties of human intercourse, for proprieties and traditional standards. And care of the exterior extended far beyond personal appearances; it concerned liveries of servants, caparisons of horses, pennons, escutcheons, and castles and manors, parks and gardens — in fact all outward things that increase the picturesque pleasures of life. Do you chance to have seen, for instance, the château near the village of Joinville that Claude de Guise built after coming from Lorraine to France? Fancy it peopled by such bright figures as you see in *Books of*

Hours, and you will understand how its spacious elegance, its handsome proportions, its pilasters and wall spaces, its grace of balustrade and gable, when tricked out and adorned by lords and ladies clad in purple mantles, green doublets, vermilion bodices, orange stomachers, by servants in piebald liveries, by cloth of gold and silver, might well be deemed to add more to the sum of human happiness than a row of model cottages, with stocked larders and sanitary plumbing, in the neighboring village.

The outward appointments of a gentleman showed nobility and excellence, but his qualities within were also expected to portray nobility and excellence. His character, — I am speaking of the ideal member of the Guild, for all wool merchants do not always sell fine wool, nor all apothecaries always furnish wholesome drugs, nor all stonemasons always build everlasting walls, — his character was based on the cardinal virtues, Fortitude, Temperance, Prudence, and Justice. And as for accomplishments and characteristics that may be acquired, the Guild prescribed: for the body, quickness, dexterity, control of the limbs, development of the muscles; and for the mind, cultivation of the humanities, of the arts, of knowledge of whatever mankind has done to make our world more beautiful and life pleasanter. And, very much as other guilds were held to justify themselves by what they contributed to society, the Guild of Gentlemen was thought to justify itself, first by public service in war and in government, and secondly by what it did to uphold the higher human values, as by its demonstration of how all human intercourse may be embellished, how conduct may become a fine art, how animal mating may be idealized by courtly love, how speech may be more than purely utilitarian, and so forth. Such, in a general way, were the fruits of civilization, which the Guild of Gentlemen gathered and contributed to the public good.

But, some may say, these fruits of human experience gathered by gentlemen are not the best and ripest fruits; there is religion, there is poetry, there is music. That is true; but they that till the garden of religion are saints, not gentlemen; they that write poetry are poets; they that compose music are musicians. The Guild of Gentlemen had a lesser, but yet an important, function. It gathered together, mixing them with other things, — alloys, if you will, — the works of the saint, of the poet, of the musician; coördinated them; adapted them to its own needs and to the needs of others (persons, both they and the others, of less lofty, less intense, but wider interests), and made of the whole an intellectual, æsthetic, social,

and physical culture, which one generation handed
on to the next; and so prepared a broader, more
universal, foundation, a more disinterested and
just appreciation, for all the several elements that
entered into this culture, than if these various sec-
tions of the human spirit had been left separate and
distinct. It enforced, or attempted to enforce, a
system of civilized opinions, derived from tradition, and shaped by experience and by that detach-
ment from the pressure of immediate needs that
only privilege and leisure can procure. It defined
and enacted the code of honor. It set up permanent principles, from which one generation may
have veered to the right and the next to the left;
principles which at one time needed to be empha-
sized and at another passed lightly over; principles that from time to time have challenged criticism and provoked debate, but in the long run
have answered criticism and survived debate; principles that inspire loyalty, that offer a haven of
refuge, a citadel of escape, a secular sanctuary.

I am aware that this definition differs from
Thomas Dekker's definition of "the first true gentleman that ever breathed"; or that of the Stoics,
who deemed a sage a gentleman; or of the army,
which classifies every officer as a gentleman. I am
merely trying to give the definition of the members of the Guild as they saw themselves — no

doubt with bias, but not more bias than enters into the judgment of any one guild or class about itself or about another. Outsiders have always, throughout the centuries, directed their attention not to the good which the Guild did, but to its pleasures and privileges, just as outsiders — social-ists, humanitarians, democrats — do to-day; but the members themselves fixed their eyes upon the accomplishment by the Guild and believed that it rendered civic services that in benefit to society constituted more than an equivalent of whatever their privileges may have cost society. And they explained and justified to themselves their opin-ion somewhat in this way. I quote a spokesman of seventy years ago (Bailey on *Representative Government*, cited by Walter Bagehot): —

"There is an unconquerable and to a certain extent . . . a beneficial proneness in man to rely on the judgment and authority of those who are elevated above him in rank and riches. From the irresistible associations of the human mind, a feeling of respect and deference is entertained for a superior in station which enhances and exalts all his good qualities, gives more grace to his move-ments, more force to his expressions, more beauty to his thoughts, more wisdom to his opinions, more weight to his judgment, more excellence to his virtues. . . . Hence the elevated man of society

[9]

will always maintain an ascendency which, without any direct exertion of influence, will affect the result of popular elections". . . and, as the Guild would have added if questioned, will affect many other matters of consequence in social life as well. And, as I like to cite advocates of an earlier generation, who lived while the Guild was still what our newspapers call "a going concern," I will quote on this one point of the Guild's political services — for I shall take up other points later — a passage from Lecky, in the *History of England in the Eighteenth Century:* —

A government of gentlemen may be and often is extremely deficient in intelligence, in energy, in sympathy with the poorer classes. It may be shamefully biassed by class interests, and guilty of great corruption in the disposal of patronage, but the standard of honour common to the class at least secures it from the grosser forms of malversation, and the interests of its members are indissolubly connected with the permanent well being of the country. Such men may be guilty of much misgovernment, and they will certainly, if uncontrolled by other classes, display much selfishness, but it is scarcely possible that they should be wholly indifferent to the ultimate consequences of their acts, or should divest themselves of all sense of responsibility or public duty. When other things are equal, the class which has most to lose and least to gain by dishonesty will exhibit the highest level of integrity. When other things are equal the class whose interests are most permanently and seriously bound up with those of the nation is likely to be the most careful guardian of the national welfare. When other things are equal, the class which has most leisure and most means of instruction will, as a whole, be the most intelligent. Besides this, the tact, the refinement, the reticence, the conciliatory tone of thought and manner characteristic of gentlemen are all peculiarly valuable in public men, whose chief task is to reconcile conflicting pretensions and to harmonize jarring interests.

And Lecky is borne out by the history of the English patricians from the time of Simon de Montfort down through the nineteenth century. However, I intend to travel farther afield than English history in order to support my definition by instances; but first I will go more into detail with regard to a gentleman's traits, to his privileges and duties; and I will begin with his duties, his obligations, for the gentleman's uppermost thought has been *noblesse oblige*.

II

A GENTLEMAN'S OBLIGATIONS

IN early times, and indeed all through the ages, the first obligation of a gentleman was to be a leader in battle — in times of war to be foremost in the field and in peace to busy himself with preparations for war. A gentleman knew how to handle weapons, and to teach his men how to handle them; he imposed discipline and drill upon them; he summoned them to assemble, and set them an example of valor, of devotion to the tribe, or state, or nation, to which they all belonged. He was also a leader in civil matters, in government, in framing and executing policy; he studied social needs, investigated the experience of the past, conferred with his equals and enacted the laws. He was a magistrate, and performed functions necessary to the maintenance of public order, and, of necessity, he was concerned with all duties that spring from the possession of property. The habit of command, the familiarity of responsibility, the association of personal interests with the interests of the state, made the gentleman ready and eager to return to society an equivalent to what he received.

Beside rendering such active services in war and politics, — which, indeed, I think we may take for granted, — the Guild of Gentlemen paid its debt to society for privileges received in another and hardly less important way. Its members constituted a body of persons who sympathized, as spectators, audience, readers, with the productions, and efforts at production, of men with special talents — poets, musicians, artists; they lent a ready ear, tendered encouragement, applauded success, criticized defects, and, as dry leaves catch a spark, preserved flashes of genius from passing into nothingness. They were more than useful, they were necessary; not merely as patrons, — such as Mæcenas, Leo X, Fouquet, for instance, — but to provide a motive for the artist, for no piper pipes for long if there are none to listen, no shepherd composes madrigals if there is no shepherdess to blush with pleasure. The Parthenon would not have been built had not the eupatridæ already established principles of harmony, proportion, measure, which descended to the so-called democracy of Pericles as an obligatory tradition, trained Pheidias, Iktinos, and their co-workers, and enabled Athenians of place and power to respect modules, to enjoy the delicacies of curve, the play of shadow upon pillar and cornice. The glories of Notre Dame de Chartres would never have been embodied in arch, column, and pier, in statue and window, if the senses of Thibaut de Chartres, Raoul de Courtenay, Pierre Mauclerc, Queen Blanche of Castile, Thibaut of Champagne, and such, had not been educated, disciplined, and refined. The literatures of Greece, of Rome, of the Italian Renaissance, of the Siècle de Louis XIV, of Castile in its great days, of all periods distinguished by proportion, measure, and restraint, are builded on the appreciation of a class of cultivated gentlemen. So, by this service of receptivity, the Guild of Gentlemen has contributed its part. It was, of course, highly paid, by privilege, leisure, and luxury, even in times when serfs and peasants were suffering from want, and the burgesses of towns were scrimping and saving; but it paid back pound for pound, florin for florin, ducat for ducat, because it held fast to the great traditions of civilization, because it cultivated and cherished tastes, feelings, standards, that raise men above the savage and the barbarian.

And by doing this it made the most important contribution towards solution of the problem of leisure. The use to which leisure should be put has always been serious, for Satan finds a God's plenty of mischief for idle hands to do, and had it not been for literature and the arts there would have been little for unoccupied men to concern themselves with, except wine, women, and prospects of war. And now that leisure is not to be the prerogative of a small class only, but the right and possession of all men, it becomes a very solemn matter indeed. Democracy and machinery will shorten the hours of labor for the multitude to such a degree that the question how to employ leisure will become more important than how to labor, and this matter, if civilization is to be preserved, cannot be left to chance. In the past, gentlemen have been the guardians of leisure; they alone possessed it, and as men for the most part take good care of their possessions, they did look after it and care for it. No doubt possessors of leisure have indulged in profligacy, in vice, in silly and stupid pastimes, but their huntings and hawkings, their jousts and pageants, their balls and their merrymakings, their dress and their trappings, not only gave them pleasure, — and pleasure is an admirable thing, — but also stimulated the sensibilities of artists and kindled their imaginations. And in the matter of leisure, the prodigal does not undo what the Admirable Crichton does; he may waste his leisure, but not that of the Admirable Crichton. One man's bad use does not hurt another man's good use. A broken jug does not empty a sound one. And the mere fact that so many famous princes have been patrons of art and literature is proof that the aristocracy of which they were the standard bearers were lovers of art and literature, for, Prospero apart, there is hardly a prince, however great his talents, who interests himself in matters that do not interest his courtiers. It is because of their interest that his interest is kindled, quickened, and encouraged; it is because they have built the pedestal that the patron prince stands so conspicuous.

Moreover, it is the very misuse of leisure that gives importance to the existence and maintenance of upright guardians of leisure. If the trained, disciplined, cultivated few, taught by tradition, and upheld by accepted standards, employ leisure in shameful and mischievous ways, what will the multitude, unexpectant heirs, intoxicated by a sudden opulence of leisure, do with their acquisition? Now, it is the professional baseball game, the prize fight, the films of Hollywood; but with an appetite for greater excitement, for sharper stimulants to the senses, to what lengths may they not go? In the past the populace has demanded bullfights, bearbaiting, gladiatorial combats, or, under the stimulus of the press, whose freedom we value so highly, war.

A GENTLEMAN'S OBLIGATIONS

In the old days when leisure was an apanage of property and privilege, a young gentleman was specially educated for the use of leisure; he was taught as a boy to take part in games and manly sports; he attended the university and studied the humanities; he went upon the grand tour in order to make acquaintance with the ways and manners of other peoples, to see their achievements in art and learn their languages, and stimulate his mind by comparison, analysis, and philosophic reflection. He was from boyhood associated with elders who had had a like education, and was naturally predisposed to be able to enter into their society, to share their experience and habits of mind. And all the time the rules of the golden mean and of self-control were held up before his eyes as guides of nearly supernatural authority. But with the multitude none of this is possible.

Even the memory of these things is passing away, and Matthew Arnold hardly sounds more modern than Cicero: "Again and again I have said how the refinement of an aristocracy may be precious and educative to a raw nation . . . how its severity and dignified freedom from petty cares may serve as a useful foil to set off the vulgarity and hideousness of that type of life which a hard middle class tends to establish, and to help people to see their vulgarity and hideousness in their true colors."

All such preaching lies unopened on library shelves because the whole subject is outmoded.

III

A GENTLEMAN'S MANNERS

AS my theme is the elimination of the gentleman that is, and for some time has been, taking place under the stress of alien forces, I will, before discussing those forces, enumerate more specifically the qualities which, according to the opinions of all generations from Homer to the end of the nineteenth century, went into the making of a gentleman, not according to their precedency in importance, but as they may happen to come to my mind.

The first note is that of manners. The old order regarded courtliness as a fine art. Even to-day travelers report that this opinion is still held in the Orient. When two Japanese gentlemen meet, they regard their meeting as an opportunity for expressing all gradations of polite satisfactions. The old order was aware how large a part casual relations play in social life, how many a little makes a mickle, how even momentary meetings with friends and acquaintances, a

[19]

lifting of the hat, a smile, a wave of the hand, a few steps out of one's way, a batch of conventional good wishes, an outward solicitude for one's health or prosperity, drop sufficient pleasantness into the fluctuating scales of ordinary existence to make the day a happy one. The old order understood how important is the outside of things. It is easy for an age that sets store by energy, by activity, by velocity, to laugh at attaching importance to the lifting of a hat, the dropping of a curtsy, the art of the tailor, of the coiffeur, of the milliner, and the various elegances of etiquette. But perhaps you well remember Velásquez's picture, "The Surrender of Breda"; how Spinola, the conquering general, bends forward to accept the tender of the city's key from the conquered Dutchman. I venture to assert that not one man in a hundred thousand knows or cares about the surrender of that little city, but that Spinola's attitude leaves its influence on every visitor to the Prado. A whole philosophy of life is delineated in that gracious portrayal of respect and sympathy. The picture represents not merely the Castilian conception of a gentleman in the days when Spanish gentlemen were the first in Europe, but one that existed, as I have said, from the time of Homer until yesterday.

A GENTLEMAN'S MANNERS

Burke says: "Nothing is more certain, than that our manners, our civilization, and all the good things which are connected with manners, and with civilization, have, in this European world of ours, depended for ages upon two principles; I mean the spirit of a gentleman and the spirit of religion." To the spirit of religion I shall refer later, but in passing I may suggest that Burke's coupling these two sentiments together was in no wise fortuitous, for the two work together, and in their essence are closely united. Neither is necessary to the other, but each is an aid. It may be said that manners, in part, are the superficial expression of religion. And the biographies of men greatly religious show that where there is holiness within there is courtesy without. There may be good manners without holiness, but there is no record of holiness without good manners.

Emerson said: "In every sense the subject of manners has a constant interest to thoughtful persons. Who does not delight in fine manners? Their charm cannot be predicted or overstated. 'T is perpetual promise of more than can be fulfilled. It is music and sculpture and picture to many who do not pretend to appreciation of those arts. It is even true that grace is more beautiful than beauty. Yet how impossible to overcome the obstacle of an unlucky temperament, and acquire good manners, unless by living with the well bred from the start."

Tennyson, too, said, — I cite him not as a poet but as a witness to contemporary beliefs, —

> For manners are not idle, but the fruit
> Of loyal nature and of noble mind.

And, indeed, it is very difficult to treat manners, the outward bearing of a man, and his character as two distinct and separate things. Rather they are the convex and the concave sides of his personality. Function shapes the organ, habitual behavior determines habitual thoughts, the outward shape begins to cast a beam on the essence within, and fine manners, good manners, gracious manners, gradually construct royal roads for action running from the brain to the members, convert them into lines of least resistance, and gradually render the human spirit within fine and good and gracious.

Cardinal Newman, who was no mean psychologist, draws this picture of a gentleman, and you can see how completely such behavior would mould the personality within: "It is almost a definition of a gentleman to say he is one who never inflicts pain. This description is both refined, and as far as it goes, accurate. He is mainly occupied in merely removing the obstacles which hinder the free and unembarrassed action of those about him; and he concurs with their movements rather than takes the initiative himself. His benefits may be considered as parallel to what are called comforts or conveniences in arrangements of a personal nature: like an easy-chair or a good fire, which do their part in expelling cold and fatigue, though nature provides both means of rest and animal heat without them. The true gentleman in like manner carefully avoids whatever may cause a jar or a jolt in the minds of those with whom he is cast; all clashing of opinion, or collision of feeling, all restraint, or suspicion, or gloom, or resentment; his great concern being to make everyone at their ease and at home. He has his eyes on all his company; he is tender towards the bashful, gentle towards the distant, and merciful towards the absurd; he can recollect to whom he is speaking; he guards against unreasonable allusions, or topics which may irritate; he is seldom prominent in conversation, and never wearisome. He makes light of favors while he does them, and seems to be receiving when he is conferring. He never speaks of himself except when compelled, never defends himself by a mere retort, he has no ears for slander or gossip, is scrupulous in imputing motives to those who interfere with him, and interprets everything for the best. He is never mean or little in his disputes, never takes unfair advantage, never mistakes personalities or sharp sayings for arguments, or insinuates evil which he dare not say out. From a long-sighted prudence, he observes the maxim of the ancient sage, that we should ever conduct ourselves toward our enemy as if he were one day to be our friend. He has too much good sense to be affronted at insults, he is too well employed to remember injuries, and too indolent to bear malice. He is patient, forbearing and resigned, on philosophical principles; he submits to pain, because it is inevitable, to bereavement because it is irreparable, and to death because it is his destiny."

Almost all of this picture of a gentleman is composed of his manners. What pleasantness there would be in life if there were many men of such manners, and is it not strange that our lovers of equality should be so blinded by humanitarian passions as not to see what a loss they inflict upon society by pooh-poohing the importance of manners, by their preaching and their practice in derision of manners.

IV

STYLE

THE second note is style. This quality is similar to that of manners, but it has a different shade of meaning, a different emphasis. Let me take the analogy of architecture. Style in architecture may signify the consistent application of a certain theory of building to the construction of an edifice, as the Greek style, the Gothic, the Renaissance, or the baroque style; but also when an edifice, in addition to its utilitarian uses, delights the eye, whether by a combination of mass and void, by interplay of light and shade, by proportion and balance, by a union of strength and delicacy, by detail and ornament, we say colloquially that it has style, and we mean that its exterior has an æsthetic value, that it gives us pleasure to look at it. This accomplishment is based on form. Whatever is noble, grand, rhythmical, subtle, whatever possesses measure or elegance, is the result of form. Form, when it is successful, has style. And let me take other analogies, as Shakespeare's description of a horse: —

IN PRAISE OF GENTLEMEN

Round-hoofed, short-jointed, fetlocks shag and long,
Broad breast, full eye, small head, and nostril wide,
High crest, short ears, straight legs, and passing strong,
Thin mane, thick tail, broad buttock, tender hide.

This horse had style; and so of a dog. You
remember Theseus's eulogy upon his hounds: —

My hounds are bred out of the Spartan kind,
So flew'd, so sanded; and their heads are hung
With ears that sweep away the morning dew;
Crook-knee'd, and dew-lapp'd like Thessalian bulls;
Slow in pursuit; but match'd in mouth like bells,
Each unto each.

These hounds had style. And in like manner
plants are selected and bred with the greatest solicitude in order to produce flowers of admired
shape, color, and odor; they are grown for their
style. If style then is desirable in flower, dog,
horse, and architecture, can it be discarded in man,
without thereby making the world a poorer place,
and life a less worth-while experience?

In literature, style used to be considered not
merely the good manners of a book, nor merely
a species of courtliness, but flesh of the flesh, bone
of the bone, of sentence, paragraph, and chapter,
no more separable from the substance than the
good points of a cocker spaniel are separable from
him. But now, in America, under the influence

of democracy, style is regarded not as an integral part of literature, but as an appendage, a badge of class, artificial finery, a relic of the old régime, an impediment to that equality which should be common to all men. This notion is, of course, a mere humanitarian illusion. Style is not an appendage, but an integral part of whatever it belongs to. Nevertheless, believers in equality are quite right to regard style as appurtenant to the aristocratical view of life.

In French prose, style continues, although but haltingly, partly because the French are a people upon whom nature has conferred taste, and partly because French prose is not handed over to the judgment of the masses; it has been kept in the aristocratic tradition by the French Academy, by the national system of literary education, by an organized respect for the French classics. In England, too, many books and some newspapers still possess style. The great heritage of English prose, bequeathed from Hooker to Jeremy Taylor, from Taylor to Clarendon, from Clarendon to Addison, from him to Burke, from Burke to Cardinal Newman, from Newman to Stevenson, and to sundry writers still living, men bred upon this heritage, or on the Greek and Latin classics, at Oxford and Cambridge — this great heritage, with its great momentum, cannot lose its authority all at once. But we in America, a people who look forward and not back, do not find this badge of class distinction to our taste. Our democratic belief in equality induces us to think that one man writes as well as another, or that anyhow writing is a practical matter, not an art. Our vocabulary has shrunk from the amplitude of the masters to the more convenient dimensions suitable to convey in the daily press the information that the multitude desires. Grammatical niceties are the hobby of the whimsical few. Dependent clauses, subjunctives, subtleties that enabled a writer to be both clear and exact, to express what critics of painting call *sfumatura;* many-faceted gradations of thought, *nuances,* and such things, have been sloughed off, they are undemocratical, alien to that comfortable ease of ready comprehension to which the humblest citizen is entitled.

However, democracy will use all the words it needs. Science, with its limited audience, will continue to employ scientific terms. The mechanical arts will continue to have their own terminology, and they, too, have a restricted class of readers. As to newspapers and ordinary books, editors and publishers, in their ambition to reach the greatest possible number of persons, find that ambition furthered by a limitation of vocabulary, so that no citizen shall be put to the inconvenience of consulting a dictionary, and furthered as well by a disregard of grammar. Besides, grammar, with its insistence upon the order of words, upon the subordination of sentences, is plainly a product of the old régime, as one may also see by such statements as that the noun *governs* the verb, whereas all words are and of right ought to be on a perfect equality. What advocates of the old system fear is that restriction upon expression, limitation upon grammatical niceties, will cramp thought. Under the old régime, an author addressed himself to the educated few, and acknowledged no duty other than the exact expression of his thought, whether following observation or imagination, but to-day his business is to cast thought into a standard mould.

V

MODESTY

ANOTHER note of the old-fashioned gentleman was reticence upon matters of sex. You remember the scene in the restaurant known as the "Cave" when Captain Costigan sang one of his "prime" songs in the presence of Colonel Newcome.

The unlucky wretch, who scarcely knew what he was doing or saying, selected one of the most outrageous performances of his *répertoire*, fired off a tipsy howl by way of overture, and away he went. At the end of the second verse the Colonel started up, clapping on his hat, seizing his stick, and looking as ferocious as though he had been going to do battle with a Pindaree. "Silence!" he roared out.

"Hear, hear!" cried certain wags at a farther table. "Go on, Costigan!" said others.

"Go on!" cries the Colonel, in his high voice, trembling with anger, "Does any gentleman say 'Go on'? Does any man who has a wife and sisters, or children at home, say 'Go on' to such disgusting ribaldry as this? Do you dare, sir, to call yourself a gentleman, and to say that you hold the king's commission, and to sit down among Christians and men of honor, and defile the ears of young boys with this wicked balderdash?"

Such reticence the present generation, full of Freudian valiancy for truth, full of the conviction that dreams are such stuff as life is made on, declares to be nonsense; matters which, in the days of my youth, Mr. Frederic Harrison printed in Latin in a footnote now stand in capital letters at the head of the chapter. Let us stand, these reformers say, for honesty and common sense; sex is sex and not to be ashamed of. Honesty is admitted, almost universally, to be an admirable quality, common sense also, and sex, as they say, is sex; but ancient tradition hung over our animal nakedness a veil of modesty and shame — qualities that did no harm and, as many thought, added a grace to life and helped to set man above the beast. Let me quote Burke again; he is talking to the *realists* of his time: —

All the decent drapery of life is to be rudely torn off. All the superadded ideas, furnished from the wardrobe of a moral imagination, which the heart owns, and the understanding ratifies, as necessary to cover the defects of our naked shivering nature, and to raise it to dignity in our estimation, are to be exploded as a ridiculous, absurd, and antiquated fashion. On this scheme of things . . . a woman is but an animal; and an animal not of the highest order. All homage paid to the sex in general as such, and without distinct views, is to be regarded as romance and folly.

It is worthy of notice that the great poets have been singularly reticent on this subject. Homer is the least Freudian of men; he accepts the fact of sex with the simplicity of a child. Vergil, too; nothing can be more delicate than the scene in the cave between Dido and Æneas. Dante, likewise; no tale of love is more restrained, or more poignant, than the recital by Francesca da Rimini, how

Amor ci condusse ad una morte.

The tragedy of Faust and Marguerite, also, is told in terms of soul and not of body. The sexual life of the animals is simple, natural, and decent.

Aristocratic tradition, tinctured by religion, supported the theory that the intellect of man should elevate sexual life into romantic love; aristocratic tradition, tinctured by romance, quoted Spenser, "Let Grylle be Grylle, and have his hoggish mind," and asked leave for those who think that life is unspeakably enriched by romantic love to follow their theory. The lot of humanity is not perfect. The mass of men lie under the curse upon Adam, "in the sweat of thy face shalt thou eat bread," and being under the law of thews and sinews rather than under the law of reason and imagination, they are exposed to the temptation of accepting sex purely on its physical basis, and over-ready to live on a naturalistic level. And now that our young intellectuals counsel loyalty to our animal ancestry, to our brutal origin, and preach a sort of sexual fundamentalism, the masses will become more and more reluctant to obey the aristocratic tradition advocated by an ever-dwindling minority — which tradition they despise, not merely because it is aristocratic and a tradition, but also because it is upheld by a minority, for the masses rely upon the judgment and sweet reasonableness of the majority.

The best hope, therefore, of an ampler air in such matters lies in some body of men who are not chained to bodily labor, not slaves to the soil, the pit, or the factory, but set free by property, leisure, and privilege to cultivate what we call spiritual values; men bred from childhood on ideas of delicacy, of refinement, of enjoyment of things of the mind and things of the spirit, and also inured to a life of physical effort by riding, boxing, boating, hunting, for if the body has its outdoor diversions, it becomes more mannerly,

more readily tamed. Such men are in these matters the workers, and all people are beneficiaries
of their labor. Some persons may suppose that
a priesthood, a clergy, a tribe of Levites, set apart
from the rough and tumble of ordinary life, would
be the best guardians of spiritual values; but a
Christian priesthood, even if it clings as close to
spiritual standards as humanitarian sympathies will
permit, — for humanitarian sympathies are with
the body and not with the spirit, — is hampered
by its devotion to a supernatural order, and so
becomes more and more estranged from common
human life, and it is precisely common human
life that needs the guidance of a specially trained
group of men. The task, if carried on at all, must
be carried on as it has been in the past, — often
lamely, I admit, but nevertheless carried on, —
by the Guild of Gentlemen.

But it appears that, in the present phase of our
civilization, reticence in the matter of sex is to go
the way of style, of manners, and a good rid-
dance it is thought to be.

VI

TASTE

ANOTHER note is that of taste. In a democracy where plebiscites decide such matters, taste fares badly. This delicate handiwork of long processes of selection, this child of privilege and slow time, over which experience, thought, logic, sensitiveness, and art have spent themselves, is so much a part and parcel of the old order that the new order, with its contempt for whatever is old, is inclined to turn up its nose and relegate it, with the humanities and suchlike, to the dust bin. But perhaps the lovers of equality are overhasty. Taste is the nurse of beauty; and love of beauty is the main distinction between man and brute. Animals eat, drink, sleep, propagate their kind, quarrel and fight very much as men do, but they do not recognize beauty — unless it be a factor in the mating season. Love of beauty is the achievement of intelligence, sensitiveness, and emotion; and as high intelligence, delicate sensitiveness, and passionate emotion are rare, so both creators of

[35]

beauty and connoisseurs of beauty are rare. In old days, when quality was valued more than quantity, when the cult of beauty was both a privilege and a duty, taste was the finger post to what the aristocracy regarded as the mind's most permanent pleasure, the love of beauty. Now all this is changed. The world lists towards democracy, equality, humanitarianism; it hardly notices the pleasures of the gifted few, and devotes itself to the satisfactions of the many; its favorite axiom is that the needs of belly and back come before the delicacies of the mind and the fastidiousness of the soul.

This solicitude for the human belly and the human back is idolatry. And the Church, or rather, I should say, the Protestant churches share in it; their ministers interpret humanitarianism in its lowest terms. How have they cheapened the great spiritual injunction: "Jesus saith to Simon Peter, Simon son of Jonas, lovest thou me more than these? He saith unto him, Yea, Lord; thou knowest that I love thee. He saith unto him, Feed my lambs. He saith to him again the second time, Simon son of Jonas, lovest thou me? He saith unto him, Yea, Lord; thou knowest that I love thee. He saith unto him, Feed my sheep. He saith unto him the third time, Simon son of Jonas, lovest thou me? Peter was grieved because he said unto him the third time, Lovest thou me? And he said unto him, Lord, thou knowest all things; thou knowest that I love thee." "Jesus saith unto him, Feed my sheep." Oh, the pathos of it! The iteration shows that Jesus foresaw that these honest Protestant clergymen would be literal-minded men. Or, perhaps, they are intellectuals, and so do not read the Gospel of Saint John.

The centre of human gravity has shifted. The old spiritual values — contemplation, meditation, the commandments of self-control and self-improvement — are cast aside; the humanities, with their exaltation of the cardinal virtues, Fortitude, Temperance, Prudence, and Justice, thrown overboard; and if this be so, — and it is so, — if the humanities are neglected for scientific specialization, religion neglected for gratifications of the humanitarian herd instinct, the Guild of Gentlemen metaphorically hurried *à la lanterne*, who then will maintain the sacred cult of beauty, who uphold the nobler values of life?

Beauty must not be left to chance; it requires a body of guardians devoted to its service. Æsthetes are not to be trusted, for æsthetes seek to detach beauty from the general stuff of human experience, to isolate it, and fence it about; they surround it with a priesthood of their own, praise

it in an esoteric liturgy and seek to render the cult
exclusively their own. The task is, and always
has been, to bring beauty out of its sacred enclosure
into ordinary life; its servitors should be in and
of this workaday world, and understand the workaday world's need of beauty; they should mix
in all the interests of life and take the cult of
beauty with them. This task, under the old order, the Guild of Gentlemen assumed and, in a
not inadequate measure, performed. Even in the
full flood of popular enthusiasm for democracy,
James Russell Lowell said: "I see as clearly as
any man possibly can, and rate as highly, the value
of wealth, and of hereditary wealth, as the security
of refinement, the feeder of all those arts that en-
noble and beautify life, and as making a country
worth living in" (1884). And, speaking of England, Lecky says: "In addition to many states-
men, orators or soldiers — in addition to many
men who have exhibited an admirable adminis-
trative skill in the management of vast proper-
ties and the improvement of numerous depend-
ents, the English aristocracy has been extremely
rich in men who, as poets, historians, art critics,
linguists, philologists, antiquaries or men of science, have attained a great or, at least, a respect-
able eminence."

This testimony as to the artistic activity of the aristocracy is but one half of the matter; it is the other half that I lay emphasis on — not upon the activities of gentlemen in service of things of the mind and of the spirit, but upon their receptivity, their appreciation, their service as disseminators. This body of gentlemen, — bred upon privilege, segregated from their fellows by possession of property, each going his own way, but all coöperating in the common task by exchange of ideas, by emulation, by mutual encouragement, by a sense of moral obligation, — this body of gentlemen prepared a spiritual home, wherein they received, welcomed, and applauded men of genius, men of talent, creators of beauty, whatever their origin, like the landlord of an old-fashioned hostelry. They regarded beauty as a royal element in nature, bringing its own authority, approved by reason, justified by experience, subservient to life as a whole, and holding out to poor humanity the best hope of a brighter day in some to-morrow. They, — I am speaking of ideal gentlemen, — having been disciplined to these ends in youth, were ready to hail all the arts — to take delight in beauty of sound, from a Mozart or a Brahms; delight in beauty of line and color, in pictures by Simone Martini, Poussin, Watteau, Gainsborough; delight in beauty of plane and contour in Praxiteles and Scopas, in Donatello, Falconet, or Mestrovic;

in builded beauty of stone, or brick, or wood, or
steel, whatever displayed the strength, the repose,
the elegance of harmony, measure, proportion,
ornament.

Such appreciation was passed along from gentleman to gentleman, modified by this one, enhanced
by that, all the time acquiring authority from general acceptance, and so, become a dogma, like
that of the value of courage, of good breeding,
of manly sports, affected daily life in the most
common things at every turn. In Homeric times
gentlemen delighted in the decoration of a shield,
reminiscent, it might be, of that which Hephaistos
wrought for Achilles, in the carving on the prow
of a galley, in the ornamentation of a chariot, in
the art and embroidery of garments; and so it has
been in all subsequent generations; gentlemen have
called upon artists to enrich the materials in all
familiar things, — statues, pictures, tapestries, furniture, vases, goblets, dishes, — teaching the eye
that beauty lurks in curve and contour, in texture
and color, in proportion and contrast. And not
in little things only. There were cathedrals;
William of Sens, l'Abbé Suger, Evrard de Fouil-
loi, and a long line of prelates, princes, lords and
ladies, took infinite pains with architectural plans
and projects, with vault and apse and radiating
chapels, with images, *entrelacs*, zigzags, lozenges,

flowers and leaves; they studied Christian sarcophagi, Byzantine ivories, and Persian textiles. There were châteaux, — François Premier is described as an artist to his finger tips, — castles, mansions, manor houses; there were pleasure domes and pleasaunces; there were parks and gardens.

You remember how Bacon describes a princelike garden: "For Gardens, the contents ought not well to be under Thirty Acres of Ground; and to be divided into three parts; a Greene in the entrance; a Heath or Desart in the Going forth; and the Maine Garden in the midst; Besides Alleys on both sides. And I like well, that Foure Acres of Ground, be assigned to the Greene; Six to the Heath; Foure and Foure to either Side; and Twelve to the Maine Garden. The Greene hath two pleasures; The one because nothing is more Pleasant to the Eye than Greene Grasse kept finely shorne; the other, because it will give you a faire Alley in the midst, by which you may go in front upon a Stately Hedge, which is to inclose the Garden." And so on; the mere list of flowers, following in turn the sequence of the seasons, fills the air with their imagined sweetness; they constitute, as he says, a *Ver Perpetuum*. Such princelike gardens, the châteaux of the Loire, the cathedrals of the Ile-de-France, do not spring from the proletariat, but from the desires of the Guild of Gentlemen.

All sorts of things, great and small, inherited from the past testify that the creation of beauty and the appreciation of beauty have been appurtenances of privilege.

VII

PRIVACY

ANOTHER note of the Guild I am describing is a love of privacy. Nothing, perhaps, is less sympathetic to democracy, to lovers of equality and fraternity, than the liberty of a man to live by himself. Equality loves company and is exasperated by any aristocratic aloofness. The old notion, whether concerning things physical or things moral, of a walled garden, of "sporting your oak," of seclusion, retirement, solitude, has gone. What used to be considered the inalienable right of a man to keep himself and his affairs to himself is his no longer. It has not only ceased to be a right, but it has become a wrong done to the public.

If an *aggressive* editor drops but a hint, on the instant his reporters and photographers leap over walls, peek through keyholes, push doors open, scramble in windows, creep, intrude, and climb into anything that is creepable, intrudable, or climbable, rush into bedrooms, crawl under beds, try the plumbing in the bathroom, tip the dirty-clothes basket upside down, and all because it is alleged that the sovereign people would be amused to know what a quiet, shy, retiring man may chance to busy himself about; for the public regards a quiet, shy, retiring man as it does some beast in the zoo, which has been tracked with infinite pains and pulled out of its hole by curators of natural history museums, in lands beyond strange seas. Publicity is the cry. A youth that aims to be of note is hurried to the housetops, given a loud speaker, and bidden to bawl out his qualifications; and universities give prizes for what they call *results* in the arts of advertising. Perhaps no factor at work in the transformation of our civilization is so potent as publicity; it acts like a surging tide upon a shelving beach that rubs and smooths and rounds off the many-faceted pebbles into the similarity of boys' marbles.

This all-pervasive force acts everywhere; it acts upon religion. I am told that Professor Whitehead and Dean Inge believe that religion is what the individual does with his own solitude, that if you are never solitary you are never religious. Thomas à Kempis, in his chapter on the love of silence and solitude, says: "The greatest Saints avoided the company of men, when they could, and chose to live in privacy with God. . . . He

that means to attain to the inner life and things
of the spirit, let him imitate Jesus and turn aside
from the multitude. . . . If thou wishest the
prick of repentance in thy heart enter thy closet
and shut out the noises of the world, as it is written, Commune with your own heart upon your
bed and be still (Psalms IV. 4)."

If this be so, then the loss of privacy, which
means the loss of solitude, is a hard blow at religion, not merely revealed religion, but what the
two distinguished men to whom I referred call
real religion, or the essence of religion. It is
natural enough, therefore, and quite excusable,
that ministers and deacons and such, expelled as it
were from their natural abode, should become
humanitarians, and what not. There even exists,
I am told, a sect of people who hold "house parties
. . . where spontaneous disclosures of the most
private experiences of the spiritual [*sic*] life could
occur quite naturally . . . where retreats and in-
formal intimate discussions for sharing personal
discoveries are commonplace features of religious
[*sic*] work."

And as it is with privacy and solitude, so it is
with reserve. The true democrat lives in a glass
house, wears his heart on his sleeve, turns his
wallet of experiences inside out, publishes his daily
doings, his triumphs, his hopes, the incidents of his

[45]

amorous life, and feels defrauded whenever an old-fashioned man refuses to do the same. If your heart were in the right place, would you keep your curtains down and your front door shut? The old adage that a man's house is his castle bears all the marks of the old régime. A castle, to be sure! The very emblem of aristocracy, pride, privilege, privacy, and inequality.

And so, privacy, once regarded as the basis of civilization, of religion, of man's comradeship with God, is shown the door, together with manners, taste, style, and modesty. And there remain these three, Liberty, Fraternity, and Equality, and the greatest of these is Equality. I said, thoughtlessly, that Liberty remains, but so limited, so gnawed and nibbled and curtailed, so subjected to the caprices of the masses, that the writers in the *Federalist*, the signers of the Declaration of Independence, the framers of our Constitution, if they were alive, would suggest the propriety of using some other word in its place.

VIII

THE HUMANITIES

ANOTHER note was that of education. Gentlemen of old studied the humanities. At Athens in the time of Pericles the eupatridæ studied Homer; at Rome, when Cicero lived, the young patricians studied Attic literature; in Florence, under the Medici, the *nobilissimi cavalieri toscani* studied the great Latins. And this heritage of "literature elevated above the trivialities, disengaged from the complexities, disinterested in the conflicts of contemporary life . . . awakened the æsthetic and literary sense, ennobled and refined feeling." (I quote Paul Shorey.) This classical heritage, by its intrinsic beauty and sublimity, by "the grand simplicity of its statement of the everlasting problems of life," by its disciplinary value, and by its enormous contribution of facts to the mental, moral, and historical science and to the wisdom of life, implanted, quickened, and cultivated these qualities of which I speak. Without leaving the schoolroom students traveled into distant lands that were both foreign and ancestral, golden in the romance of glorious far-off things, and grave with the reverence due to the ancient and the enduring. Professor Rand of Harvard University says, "The study of classical literature normally inspires a twofold impulse of the human spirit — reverence for the past, and the passionate desire to act worthily in the present."

This luxury of voyaging through the thought and literature of the classical world was not open to everybody, it was not open to those who must do the manual labor of the world, who are obliged to earn their own livelihood from early youth; it was the appurtenance of property and privilege. Young patricians held a monopoly of opportunity, and, however imperfectly, they justified this prerogative by upholding the law of decorum, the value of form, the abiding pleasure in beauty, the worth of manners, style, dignity, and reticence. The most impressive statement of the value of studying the classical literature that I happen to know is that by John Stuart Mill in his Rectorial address before the University of St. Andrews, and so, in spite of its length, I quote it in full: —

Even as mere languages, no modern European language is so valuable a discipline to the intellect as those of Greece and Rome, on account of their regular and complicated structure. Consider for a moment what Grammar is. It is the most elementary part of Logic. It is the beginning of the analysis of the thinking process. The principles and rules of grammar are the means by which the forms of language are made to correspond with the universal forms of thought. The distinctions between the various parts of speech, between the cases of nouns, the moods and tenses of verbs, the functions of particles, are distinctions in thought, not merely in words. Single nouns and verbs express objects and events, many of which can be cognized by the senses: but the modes of putting nouns and verbs together, express the relations of objects and events, which can be cognized only by the intellect; and each different mode corresponds to a different relation. The structure of every sentence is a lesson in logic. The various rules of syntax oblige us to distinguish between the subject and predicate of a proposition, between the agent, the action, and the thing acted upon; to mark when an idea is intended to modify or qualify, or merely to unite with, some other idea; what assertions are categorical, what only conditional; whether the intention is to express similarity or contrast, to make a plurality of assertions conjunctively or disjunctively; what portions of a sentence, though grammatically complete within themselves, are mere members or subordinate parts of the assertion made by the entire sentence. Such things form the subject matter of universal grammar; and the languages which teach it best are those which have the most definite rules, and which provide distinct forms for the greatest number of distinctions in thought, so that

[49]

if we fail to attend precisely and accurately to any of these, we cannot avoid committing a solecism in language. In these qualities the classical languages have an incomparable superiority over every modern language, and over all languages, dead or living, which have a literature worth being generally studied.

But the superiority of the literature itself, for purposes of education, is still more marked and decisive. Even in the substantial value of the matter of which it is the vehicle, it is very far from having been superseded. The discoveries of the ancients in science have been greatly surpassed, and as much of them as is still valuable loses nothing by being incorporated in modern treatises: but what does not so well admit of being transferred bodily, and has been very imperfectly carried off even piecemeal, is the treasure which they accumulated of what may be called the wisdom of life; the rich store of experience of human nature and conduct, which the acute and observing minds of those ages, aided in their observations by the greater simplicity of manners and life, consigned to their writings, and most of which retains all its value. The speeches in Thucydides; the *Rhetoric, Ethics,* and *Politics* of Aristotle; the Dialogues of Plato; the Orations of Demosthenes; the *Satires,* and especially the *Epistles* of Horace; all the writings of Tacitus; the great work of Quintilian, a repertory of the best thoughts of the ancient world on all subjects connected with education; and, in a less formal manner, all that is left to us of the ancient historians, orators, philosophers, and even dramatists, are replete with remarks and maxims of

THE HUMANITIES

singular good sense and penetration, applicable both to
political and to private life: and the actual truths we find
in them are even surpassed in value by the encouragement
and help they give us in the pursuit of truth.   Human
invention has never produced anything so valuable, in the
way both of stimulation and of discipline to the inquiring
intellect, as the Dialectic of the ancients, of which many
of the works of Aristotle illustrate the theory, and those
of Plato exhibit the practice.   No modern writings come
near to these, in teaching, both by precept and example,
the way to investigate truth, on those subjects, so vastly
important to us, which remain matters of controversy,
from the difficulty or impossibility of bringing them to a
directly experimental test.   To question all things; never
to turn away from any difficulty; to accept no doctrine
either from ourselves or from other people without a
rigid scrutiny by negative criticism, letting no fallacy, or
incoherence, or confusion of thought, slip by unperceived;
above all, to insist upon having the meaning of a word
clearly understood before using it, and the meaning of a
proposition before assenting to it; — these are the lessons
we learn from the ancient dialecticians.   With all this
vigorous management of the negative element, they inspire no skepticism about the reality of truth, or indifference to its pursuit.   The noblest enthusiasm, both for
the search after truth and for applying it to its highest
uses, pervades these writers, Aristotle no less than Plato,
though Plato has incomparably the greater power of
imparting those feelings to others.   In cultivating, therefore, the ancient languages as our best literary educa-

tion, we are all the while laying an admirable foundation for ethical and philosophical culture. In purely
literary excellence — in perfection of form — the pre-
eminence of the ancients is not disputed. In every department which they attempted, and they attempted
almost all, their composition, like their sculpture, has
been to the greatest modern artists an example, to be
looked up to with hopeless admiration, but of inap-
preciable value as a light on high, guiding their own
endeavors. In prose and in poetry, in epic, lyric, or
dramatic, as in historical, philosophical, and oratorical
art, the pinnacle on which they stand is equally eminent.
I am now speaking of the form, the artistic perfection
of treatment; for, as regards substance, I consider modern
Poetry to be superior to ancient, in the same manner,
though in a less degree, as modern Science: it enters
deeper into nature. The feelings of the modern mind
are more various, more complex and manifold, than
those of the ancients ever were. The modern mind is,
what the ancient mind was not, brooding and self-
conscious; and its meditative self-consciousness has discovered depths in the human soul which the Greeks and
Romans did not dream of, and would not have understood. But what they had got to express, they expressed
in a manner which few even of the greatest moderns
have seriously attempted to rival. It must be re-
membered that they had more time, and that they wrote
chiefly for a select class, possessed of leisure. To us
who write in a hurry for people who read in a hurry,
the attempt to give an equal degree of finish would be

loss of time. But to be familiar with perfect models is not the less important to us because the element in which we work precludes even the effort to equal them. They show us at least what excellence is, and make us desire it, and strive to get as near to it as is within our reach. And this is the value to us of the ancient writers, all the more emphatically, because their excellence does not admit of being copied, or directly imitated. It does not consist in a trick which can be learned, but in the perfect adaptation of means to ends. The secret of the style of the great Greek and Roman authors, is that it is the perfection of good sense.

I have quoted this admirable passage at length, a passage rendered more impressive from the fact that Mill was a utilitarian and in his way a staunch believer in democracy, because it makes clear how important the humanities are, and how impossible it would be to preserve them except by "a select class, possessed of leisure." If any American public-school curriculum includes the classics, it is illogical, for the classics do not conduce to the practical ends for which the public-school curriculum was established; they do not help in housing, clothing, feeding families, nor do they add to the zest and enthusiasm of a ball game, nor are they necessary for the understanding of motion pictures. They are part and parcel of class education; and if the class is submerged in the masses, the study of the classics will go, also.

IX

UPHOLDERS OF CONVENTION

SUCH, then, are the notes that characterized gentlemen as individuals. As a Guild, collectively, gentlemen also exercised important social functions, they were the administrators of convention.

Civil society, as Plato says, arises out of the needs of mankind; no individual is self-sufficing; all men have many wants and many people are needed to supply those wants; one takes an assistant for one purpose and another for another, and when the assistants and partners are gathered in one habitation, the body of inhabitants is termed a state. But, in a state, wants jostle one another, ambitions clash, greed falls foul of greed, and from these janglings and quarrels rises the need of law (*Republic*, II), and from them also rises the need of convention. Law fences in the area of social life, sets barriers on this side and on that, marking off compartments, defining civil rights, crimes, torts, contractual duties, the ownership of property, and all the fundamental matters on which society rests. Law is rigid, austere, and impersonal; it is in the hands of lawyers, men of special education and training; it is administered by judges, juries, sheriffs, with all the paraphernalia of courts and jails, and it is supported by the organized power of the state. But, as we all know, society is controlled by social conventions quite as much as by law. The sanction behind the law is physical force, the sanction behind convention is social disapproval. Convention, as it were, controls the suburbs and the country districts, it regulates matters disregarded by the law, but which, nevertheless, fill a great part in our ordinary lives.

Convention prescribes a man's behavior in a hundred daily matters, some of which Plato enumerated in *The Republic:* "I mean such things as these: — when the young are to be silent before their elders; how they are to show respect to them by sitting down and rising up; what honor is due to parents; what garments or shoes are to be worn; the mode of dressing the hair; deportment and manners in general." These are the things that make most of the warp and woof of daily life. There is the morning salutation at breakfast, when a clouded brow or a surly silence will spoil the day; there is the proper sequence of dishes, fruit first or last, cracking the eggshell at the large or little end, behavior to the servant — whether in the English fashion as a block of animated wood, or in the French fashion as a garrulous friend; and outdoors, of whom or when one shall take the wall; who shall make the first call, the stranger or the old inhabitant. These, and suchlike, are matters that, if undetermined, if left to chance and the moment, cause friction; and friction begets heat, heat a flame, flame a fire, fire a conflagration.

Over these matters of convention, over manners and behavior not regulated by law, there must be tutors and masters, officers and magistrates; and these were provided, under the old régime, by the Guild of Gentlemen. As I have said, this Guild did not constitute a class, though the group partook of the character of a class; it was rather a club, open to all persons furnished with the qualities prescribed by the constitution of the club; and this perhaps is the origin of the phrase, soon distorted from its proper meaning, *persons of quality*. Strictly speaking, the mere fact of birth would not entitle admission to this club, but parents of social position, of wealth, of leisure, for the most part endeavored to educate their children in such manner as to make them eligible as a matter of course. The requirements did not necessarily include the four cardinal virtues, nor kindness, generosity, pity, although most of the requisite clubbable qualities have their roots in these virtues and derive their nourishment therefrom. Nevertheless, the virtues were present in generous measure, or the Guild would have perished long since, but certain outer traits were necessarily present also.

You remember in *Twelfth Night*, after Viola said, "I am a gentleman," Olivia's comment was, "I 'll be sworn thou art. Thy tongue, thy face, thy limbs, actions, and spirit do give thee five-fold blazons." Requisites for admission, I repeat, were courtesy, self-restraint, a nice regard to the rules of etiquette, a command of speech, an elegance of dress, a familiarity with the habits of the leisure class, a respect for appearances, for the outside of things, a desire to make the passing moment pleasurable. All these matters were governed by convention, and lay in the jurisdiction of the Guild.

There are those who take life hard, who prefer what they call an honest heart to an attractive exterior; who value men for their moral worth and are indifferent to their manners; who before the Cathedral of Rheims are more concerned with formulæ of thrust and strain than with the ornamentation of the façade or of the north portal;

who judge a picture by the perspective, a drama by its moral; who believe in eternal values; who delight in dogmas concerning righteousness, and despise appearances. Such was Jeremiah in his day, such was Thomas Carlyle in his. And of such passions are some of the clergy who address us of a Sunday morning. These men, so minded, are usually deficient in a sense of humor, in æsthetic appreciation, in a recognition of the futility of ontology, in every wholesome skepticism.

It is safer to believe in what seems than in what is, in the phenomenon than in the noumenon; for appearances are much less deceitful than that which we may imagine lies behind them, and if one will but stop to think how important appearances are in daily life, one will not be surprised that past generations set so great store by the guardians of appearances. Of course the substance behind the outside is often important, most important, as when a rosy apple is rotten within; but to one passing a tree of beautiful rosy apples, on which the sunlight and the shadows of the leaves frisk and flirt, the state of the pulp of the apples is indifferent. So is it in a thousand matters in daily life. I walk through a village: I see proper gardens, fresh-painted houses, shining windowpanes, polished knockers and door handles — what to me is untidiness and frowziness within?

I dine abroad: I care not for the character of the cook, so that his viands be savorous, nor of the butler, if he will be careful not to stir up the lees in the Montrachet and will see to it that the wine is of the proper temperature; I care little for the private lives of my companions, if only their talk is good and the ladies' dresses display the charm of color, propriety, and elegance, and the men's clothes betray that their tailors recognize that the tailor's craft is an art. The very fact that the substance within is important renders the exterior of consequence.

Yes, the outside is of immense consequence in the enjoyment of life. Of this outside the Guild of Gentlemen would be the natural guardians; they enact tacit regulations, they prescribe the sorts of behavior suitable to various occasions; they stand upright on their feet, they sit erect in their chairs, and in a conversation they listen as much as they talk. Most multifarious matters come within their ken; let me take an instance of a dreadful state of things, universal in America to-day, due to the absence of the Guild's influence. Drive your motor anywhere in the country; every hundred yards, or less, there is an advertisement of "eats," "nite sleeps," "home kumforts," "walk inns," and such, beside an infinite number of cordial counsels to buy, use, investigate, try, and prove the invaluable qualities of cocoa, whiskey, motor oil, milk-fed turkeys, mother's jams, and other physical or moral necessities *ad infinitum*. Such expressions of democracy would have been sternly suppressed, for the Guild of Gentlemen, sentimentally bred, æsthetic epicureans, preferred the sight of trees and hillsides, of brook and meadow. So, too, with the democratic habit of strewing the Sunday newspaper, after carefully separating its scores of sheets, over the lea.

Fine feathers, it is said, do not make fine birds, but fine feathers do not prevent birds from being fine, nor do foul, sluttish feathers necessarily make fine birds. A man may be valiant, truthful, intelligent, public-spirited, prudent, temperate, and just, and yet wear good clothes, exhibit fine manners, speak correct English, and have an agreeable voice. Our ancestors believed that the outside of men, their appearance, their manners, were matters of great value in this dubious adventure of life, and so they respected the guardians of appearances.

And now that I have indicated in a general way the qualities that marked the Gentleman, the duties incumbent upon him, and his principal functions, I will proceed to the various aspects of him that have received special emphasis in different generations from the time of the ancient Greeks down to the beginning of this century, in pursuance of my purpose to discover what truth, if any, there may have been in that ancient idea that gentlemen were of benefit to society at large.

PART TWO

The conception of a gentleman through the ages

X

THE HOMERIC GENTLEMAN

THE fundamental notion behind the acceptance of privileges is that the members of
the Guild of Gentlemen must, as we say, pay
their way, must feel what is called the sense of
noblesse oblige, a sentiment that has never been
better expressed than by a passage in the *Iliad.*
Two of the Trojan allies from Lykia, Sarpedon
and Glaukos, take part in Hector's assault upon
the Grecian camp. Sarpedon says to Glaukos:
"Glaukos, wherefore have we twain the chiefest
honor, — seats of honor and messes, and full cups
in Lykia, and all men look on us as gods? And
wherefore hold we a demesne by the banks of
Xanthos, a fair demesne of orchard-land, and
wheat-bearing tilth? Therefore now it behoveth
us to take our stand in the first rank of the Lykians,
and encounter fiery battle, that certain of the well-
corseleted Lykians may say, 'Verily our kings that
rule Lykia be no inglorious men, they that eat fat
sheep, and drink the choice wine honey-sweet;

nay, but they are also of excellent might, for they war in the foremost ranks of the Lykians.' . . . Now — for assuredly ten thousand fates of death do every way beset us, and these no mortal may escape nor avoid — now let us go forward, whether we shall give glory to other men, or others to us." . . . And the twain went straight forward, leading the great host of the Lykians.[1]

In those days there was no democracy. The *Iliad* is the story of chieftains; the many serve but as supernumeraries, usually, if mentioned at all, as victims to display the prowess of adversary chieftains. In the *Odyssey*, too, society is that of small communities ruled by kings and chiefs, who with their families and friends constituted the dominant class; the common people, whether serfs or slaves, were of no account. This domination brought with it class behavior. The rulers might have rested content to distinguish themselves from the plebeians by power and enjoyment, but they chose to distinguish themselves, also, by manners.

One has but to read a scene or two from the *Odyssey* to perceive the value set upon manners, upon duties prescribed by convention. You will remember how Telemachos left Ithaca to seek news of his father. In company with a son of Nestor, he arrives at the palace of Menelaos in

[1] Lang's translation.

Lacedæmon, at the time when Menelaos is giving a feast in honor of his daughter's betrothal. The whole affair is such as might have taken place in any of these centuries at the country house of a prosperous gentleman. One of the household, who acts as a sort of major-domo, meets the two strangers at the door, and, uncertain what to do, doubtless because there were so many guests already, goes and announces their arrival to Menelaos, and asks whether he shall invite them in or send them elsewhere.

Menelaos was greatly vexed: "Etoneos, you used not to be a fool, but now you talk like a silly child. You and I have often partaken of the hospitality of other men on our way home [from Troy]. . . . Unharness the horses and fetch the men here directly to take part in the feast." Etoneos hurried to obey. The horses were put in the stables and fed, the guests taken to the bath, given fresh clothes, seated at table beside Menelaos, and bountifully served with food. Menelaos said: "Help yourselves to the viands and be welcome, and after supper I shall ask who you are, for the breed of your sires has not suffered in you; you are the sons of sceptred kings nurtured by Zeus; for churls could not beget sons like you."

You perceive the undemocratic spirit of the

time. The phrase, "son of a sceptred king nurtured by Zeus," means what Sir Walter Scott would have called a gentleman. The guests ate and drank all they wanted; then Telemachos, a little abashed by the unaccustomed magnificence of the palace, called his friend's attention to it, and whispered that it must be like the halls of Zeus on Olympus.

Menelaos overheard the words and said: "Dear boys, no man could vie with Zeus. His palace and his furnishings are divine; but of men some might vie with me in wealth, or perhaps not. . . . Would that I had but a third part of what I have, and that those men were alive who perished in the broad plains of Troy. And yet, though I often sit in my halls, weeping and sorrowing for them all . . . despite my grief I mourn not so much for all the others, as for one only who makes me hate sleep and food when I think of him; for none of the Achæans toiled so much as Odysseus toiled and endured. Woe was allotted to him as his portion and to me unforgettable grief for him. He is gone so long, and we do not know whether he is alive or dead. The old man Laertes, I suspect, is mourning him, and loyal Penelope, and Telemachos whom he left a newborn infant in his home." [1]

[1] A. T. Murray's translation.

THE HOMERIC GENTLEMAN

Telemachos shed tears when he heard of his father, and tried to conceal them by holding up his cloak, but Menelaos perceived the tears and guessed the truth. While he was wondering what he had better say, Helen, recaptured after so much toil, entered the room. She was most emphatically a lady, a *grande dame*. She looked like Artemis. Her attendants came with her; one placed her chair, a second her rug, a third pushed up her silver basket that ran on wheels; her wool and her distaff were given to her, and a footstool set for her feet. She at once recognized Telemachos as looking exactly like his father; Menelaos agreed, and revealed their thoughts. Nestor's son then said: "This young man is indeed the son of Odysseus, as you say. But he is modest and feels shyness in his heart to speak up on his first arrival in your presence, for he and I delight in your voice as in that of a god's."

They were all greatly moved by the situation. Helen wept. Telemachos wept, Menelaos wept, and even Nestor's son could not keep a dry eye. They talked of Odysseus, of Antilochos, another son of Nestor's, killed in the war, of sorrow and so on, till Menelaos counseled them to lay grief aside and come to supper. Then Helen took one of the drugs of healing given her by an Egyptian lady and dropped it into the wine. This drug

[69]

calmed all pain and quarrel, and brought forget-fulness of every ill. He that drank of the wine, in which it was mingled, would not shed a tear, no matter what hideous misfortune might befall him.

This I take to be an allegory to indicate the value of perfect breeding. All privileges were Helen's, — high birth, beauty beyond that of mortal women, luxury, great adventure, foreign travel, — and by means of these she was enabled to bring into a sorrowful company so sweet a charm that all sorrow was at once forgotten. Such was the notion of manners, of high breeding, of style, in Homeric days.

Privilege, especially in the eyes of those that do not possess it, may seem an evil thing; and a cry for equality has swept the world, and silenced those who knew, or suspected, or imagined, that there were others above them. The one thing that equality has not affected is Nature, who continues to deal out unequal gifts according to her own whimsical fancy; and since human society is sprung of Nature, is a part of Nature, it may prove that this popular rebellion against the law of our common mother is not wholly wise.

XI

ACCORDING TO PLATO AND ARISTOTLE

A GENTLEMAN, I repeat again, was a product of privilege. His character, however,
was based on the accepted virtues, for if he had
not won the approbation of society in the weight-
ier matters, he would not have been able to per-
suade it of the seriousness of those other human
qualities that I have been describing. Nevertheless, possession of all the virtues was not enough
to entitle their possessor to enter the Guild. One
never thinks of Habakkuk, John the Baptist,
Epictetus, Martin Luther, or Calvin as gentlemen;
they were prophets, saints, heroes, if you like, but
not gentlemen. It was the possession of other
qualities — a modest dignity, self-control, a care
of manners, an appreciation of style — that, in ages
past, caused the type to be regarded as beneficial
to society. This was particularly true of the Athenians in the fourth century before Christ. The
polity of Athens was democratical, inasmuch as all

free citizens took part in the government; nevertheless, the democracy was but specious, for it rested upon slavery, and it is evident that there were various marked gradations in social life. Plato, himself, was a fastidious gentleman.

In that poetical fantastic dialogue, *The Republic*, Socrates describes a state as it should be. I refer you to Jowett's translation; the dialogue is surely included in every academic list of books that ought to be read. In this utopian state there are to be guardians, who are primarily warriors, as gentlemen have always been until the establishment of standing armies; but they must also be lovers of wisdom and knowledge and unite in themselves philosophy and spirit and swiftness and strength; they must be educated, body and mind: the body by gymnastics and various active exercises, the mind by literature and music — that is, by those disciplines over which the Muses preside. They should imitate, from youth onward, such characters as are courageous, temperate, holy, and free, and turn from all kinds of illiberality or baseness. Socrates' description is charming, and he gives loose rein to his fancy. He talks of style, says that the beauty of style and harmony and grace depends on simplicity, and that these young men must make grace and harmony their perpetual aim. Ugliness, discord, and inharmonious motion are

nearly allied to ill words and ill nature, as grace
and harmony are the twin sisters of goodness and
virtue. And then he bursts into a rhapsody concerning the effect of the arts, not merely the fine
arts, but all creative and constructive arts, whether
for good through grace and harmony, or for evil
through ugliness, meanness, and indecency.

We would not have our guardians grow up amid
images of moral deformity, as in some noxious pasture,
and there browse and feed upon many a baneful herb
and flower day by day, little by little, until they silently
gather a festering mass of corruption in their own soul.
Let our artists rather be those who are gifted to discern
the true nature of the beautiful and graceful: then will
our youth dwell in a land of health amid fair sights and
sounds, and receive the good in everything; and beauty,
the effluence of fair works, shall flow into the eye and
ear, like a health-giving breeze from a purer region, and
insensibly draw the soul from earliest years into likeness
and sympathy with the beauty of reason.

GLAUCON. There can be no nobler training than
that.

SOCRATES. And therefore musical training is a more
potent instrument than any other, because rhythm and
harmony find their way into the inward places of the
soul, on which they mightily fasten, imparting grace,
and making the soul of him who is rightly educated
graceful, or of him who is ill-educated ungraceful; and

[73]

also because he who has received this true education of
the inner being will most shrewdly perceive omissions
or faults in art and nature, and with a true taste, while
he praises and rejoices over and receives into his soul
the good, and becomes noble and good, he will justly
blame and hate the bad, now in the days of his youth,
even before he is able to know the reason why; and
when Reason comes he will recognize and salute the
friend with whom his education has made him long
familiar.

GLAUCON. I quite agree with you in thinking that
our youth should be trained in music and on the grounds
which you mention. . . .

SOCRATES. Even so, as I maintain, neither we nor
our guardians, whom we have to educate, can ever become musical until we and they know the essential forms
of temperance, courage, liberality, magnificence, and
their kindred, as well as the contrary forms, in all their
combinations, and can recognize them and their images
whenever they are found, not slighting them either in
small things or great, but believing them all to be within
the sphere of one art and study.

GLAUCON. Most assuredly.

SOCRATES. And when a beautiful soul harmonizes
with a beautiful form, and the two are cast in one mould,
that will be the fairest of sights to him who has an eye
to see it?

GLAUCON. The fairest indeed.

SOCRATES. And the fairest is also the loveliest?

GLAUCON. That may be assumed.

SOCRATES. And the man who has the spirit of harmony will be most in love with the loveliest.

For the production of such a gentleman two disciplines were necessary: liberal studies, which, as I say, he calls music; and bodily exercise, which he calls gymnastics and we call athletics. These, he says, are the principles of nurture and education, and with this he stops short of further analysis. "Where would be the use [he asks] in going into further details about their dances, their hunting or chasing with dogs, their gymnastic and equestrian contests; for these all follow the general principle." Here, then, is a plan for educating a special group of citizens quite distinct from the artisan and meaner classes, and this group is selected, trained, and educated, not for its own well-being and happiness, but for "the greatest happiness of the whole." Such an ideal is only possible on the assumption of a life wholly free from the obligation to earn one's bread by the sweat of one's brow, of a life based on all sorts of privileges, and quite impossible for the ordinary man. Plato is not, of course, describing the actual city government of Athens, but "the good and true state," the ideal state which depends upon an aristocracy not of birth but of selection, an aristocracy of gentlemen trained in virtue, in liberal studies, and in athletics — brave, temperate, lovers of grace and harmony.

And now, let us leave Plato's speculations, which are so saturated with fancy and poetry, and look at Aristotle's ideas on the same subject, for Aristotle was no poet, but a practical thinker. Aristotle describes at length what we call a gentleman and he called a seeker after the chief good — a man who has mastered the virtues, and accepts as the fundamental principle of life the rule of the golden mean. This gentleman inherits his property, and is liberal of it — neither a prodigal nor a miser. He acts as befits a man of consequence, avoiding vulgarity on the one hand and pettiness on the other, and in whatever he does asks neither how much nor how little it will cost, but considers what is noblest and most becoming to his station. He is a man of birth and rank as well as of property. He performs his duties, whether in the ceremonials of religion or in the service of the state; he pays for the performance of tragedies, for fitting out a trireme, or for doing whatever else public welfare demands. As for all matters of hospitality, if for instance there is a wedding in his family, whether as to the presents he makes, or as to the foreign guests he entertains, or as to the furnishings and ornaments of his house, in all these respects he is magnificent.

He possesses a great soul, a just self-esteem, high-mindedness, which is the regulation of the virtues, and he is covetous for honor. He values the praise of men of quality, but recks little of what common people think; as for riches he regards them but as a means to honor. He does not seek danger, but in a good cause he will risk his life; better death than dishonor. He likes to give, he is loath to receive; he bestows favors but is unwilling to accept them. He is punctilious with men of his own rank, but not so with inferiors. He cares little for small prizes, but for great ones he is all action. He values truth more than the opinions of men; he is frank and open in word and deed, and slow to lay claim to his own. He leads his life in the way he thinks best, unless it be to please a friend. He seldom expresses astonishment, and forgets injuries. He is of few words, sparing of praise and of blame; he does not gossip, does not bother himself about trifles; prefers what is splendid, though useless, to the purely utilitarian. His gait, his voice, his manner of speech, are grave, dignified, and serious; and he acknowledges decorum in conversation, for there are things that a gentleman should not say or listen to, even in times of joviality, for the joviality of an educated gentleman differs from that of a servant or of any uneducated fellow. He is affable, kindly, and watchful to say what is becoming to his self-respect and will give pleasure to those that hear, or at least not hurt their feelings, and he speaks the truth. Such is Aristotle's ideal, and this ideal rests squarely upon privilege. "It is impossible," he says, "for one who lives a mechanical or servile life to practise the virtues of conduct."

Our modern conception of a gentleman has been largely affected by Christianity and the feudal and monarchical systems, but our ideal has not changed much since the time of Plato and Aristotle. In the division of responsibility for a man's character between environment and heredity, they — partly because Athens was a nominal democracy, and partly because of the immense advantages of early training and education — laid stress upon environment, whereas, since then, believers in gentility have too hastily assumed that most of such advantages were due to birth. However that may be, throughout the whole course of the gentleman's existence you will find that he rests upon privilege and property.

XII

THE ROMAN IDEAL

THE ideal of a gentleman as drawn by Plato
was essentially concerned with what we call
sweetness and light, and that drawn by Aristotle
with aristocratic superiority. Afterwards, with the
decadence of Athens and the rise of the Stoic sect,
that ideal was modified and the element of en-
durance, of a capacity "to grin and bear it," was
grafted on. In the Roman Empire, during the
first and second centuries A.D., the Christian religion carried its supernatural consolations, of which
Nietzsche took so unfavorable a view, to the miser-
able classes, to the outcast and the slave; but
among the rich patricians the burden of unstable
empire brought anxiety, behind the rider black
care sat on the crupper, and the high-hearted Roman nobility wrapped themselves round with their
doctrines of Fortitude, Self-Control, Righteousness, and Wisdom. No type of gentleman has
ever stood higher than these stoical Roman patricians, renouncing on the one hand a life of ease,

IN PRAISE OF GENTLEMEN

of intellectual luxury, of indifference to the rising flood that was threatening the Empire, and on the other disdaining what to them was the un-Roman superstition of Christianity. Marcus Aurelius has drawn a portrait of the stoical Roman gentleman at his best in his father-in-law and adoptive father, Antoninus Pius: —

Gentleness, and unshakable firmness in decisions come to after full deliberation; no vainglory in what men call honors; love of hard work, perseverance, and a ready ear for those who have anything to propose for the common good; an unswerving determination to give to every man according to his deserts; a knowledge, got by experience, of when it is right to insist, and when to let things go; consideration for others, how he left his friends quite free to dine with him or not, and under no obligation to attend him abroad; and how men who had stayed away, constrained by some necessity or other, always found him just the same; his habit of thorough investigation at the council board, his persistency, and, further, his refusal to desist from inquiry and to rest satisfied with plausible impressions; his constancy to his friends, never fickle nor foolishly fond of them; his sufficiency unto himself on every occasion and his cheerfulness; his great foresight, and his provision for the smallest details without making a fuss about them; how he checked cheers and applause and all kinds of flattery; his watchful care over the interests of the Empire, his management of its resources, and his patience under the condemnation he was subjected to in consequence; his freedom from superstition in his attitude toward the gods; and, in his attitude toward men, no chase after popularity, no efforts to please them, no humoring the mob, but always sobriety, and steadiness; never any vulgarity or eagerness for new things.

And as to those things that contribute to the comfort of life, which fortune had heaped upon him, his use of them without arrogance and at the same time without apology, so that when they were at hand he partook of them without ostentation, and when they were not he went without. And none could say that he was a sophist or a pedant, or had any qualities of the servile courtier, but he was ripe, finished, unaffected by praise, well able to manage his own affairs and also those of other people.

Besides this, there was also his deep respect for true philosophers (he was polite even to humbugs), and yet he was not easily led by them. And also he was affable and gracious but not to excess. And he took proper care of his body (though not as a lover of physical life), and he never gave too much or too little attention to his good looks, but did just right, so that by the care he took, he hardly ever needed a doctor, or medicines, or bandages.

And above all, his deference, and freedom from envy, toward those who possessed any special accomplishment, such as oratory, or knowledge of laws, or ethics, or any other subject; and he did his best for them so that each should receive full recognition, according to his special excellence; and he always acted in accordance with traditional usages, not in order to make a display of doing so, but for the sake of preserving such usages.

Furthermore, he was not unstable or vacillating, but he liked to frequent the same places, and do the same things; and, after violent headaches, he would come back, fresh and vigorous, to his usual occupations. He had very few secrets, and those very seldom, and only about affairs of state. He displayed prudence and moderation in the management of public shows, in the construction of public works, and in distributing bounties and such matters, as a man does who looks sharp at what ought to be done, and not to the reputation that may come from what he does.

He did not frequent the baths at all hours, and he did not build for the love of building; he was not particular about what he ate, nor the texture or color of his clothes, nor the smart appearance of his slaves. His robes were made at Lorium, or his villa on the coast, but most of his clothes at Lanuvium.

There was nothing harsh about him, nor overbearing, nor violent, nor (as the saying is) did he "get into a sweat," but everything was considered each by itself (as if he were quite at leisure), without any confusion, in an orderly fashion, vigorously, and consistently. One might apply to him what was said of Socrates, that he was able both to refrain from, and to enjoy, those pleasures which most men are either weak in withstanding or overready to embrace. To be strong, to persist and not go too far, belongs to a man of perfect and unconquerable soul.[1]

[1] M. A., I, 16.

THE ROMAN IDEAL

Here surely, if anywhere, is the portrait of a great gentleman. His performance of military and political duties is taken for granted, it is implied in the word *imperator;* and here are the other qualities I enumerated — manners, style, modesty, taste, love of such privacy as is possible to the occupant of a throne, and all adorned with that ripeness which is the great gift of the humanities.

XIII

SAINT LOUIS

IF Christianity had succeeded in its substitution of the theological virtues in place of the cardinal virtues, the type of gentleman that I have attempted to describe would have disappeared, for the gentleman, so far as he is concerned with ethics, rests upon *fortitudo, justitia, prudentia,* and *temperantia,* and has, in comparison, little to do with faith, hope, and charity. It is not necessary that he should possess all those four qualities, — for Alcibiades and Henri Duc de Guise were deficient in *justitia* and *temperantia,* and yet both were great gentlemen, — but he must possess some of them, and those that he has must by their abundance make up for his deficiency in the others, as in the case of Alcibiades and Henri de Guise, who both possessed *fortitudo* in magnificent plenty. Christianity, however, did not displace the cardinal virtues; for Christianity, as we have it, did not overcome the world, but compromised by letting the world continue as it had been, on condition that the world should call itself Christian, turn temples into churches, put saints in the niches in place of the demigods, and don a cassock over the pagan tunic. Nevertheless, Christianity affected the gentleman, as you may see by the tales of the Holy Grail, far more than it did the rest of the world, and in this chapter I shall try to indicate the modifications it produced, and I hasten to say that those modifications, if they in some ways detract from the beauty of the type, in other ways enhance it.

No one has delineated the Christian gentleman better than Chaucer: —

A knight ther was, and that a worthy man,
That fro the time that he firste began
To riden out, he loved chevalrie,
Trouthe and honour, fredom and curtesie.
Ful worthy was he in his lordes werre,
And therto hadde he ridden, no man ferre,
As wel in Cristendom as in Hethenesse,
And ever honoured for his worthinesse.

This ilke worthy knight hadde ben also
Somtime with the lord of Palatie,
Agen another hethen in Turkie:
And evermore he hadde a sovereine pris.
And though that he was worthy he was wise,
And of his port as meke as is a mayde.

[85]

IN PRAISE OF GENTLEMEN

He never yet no vilanie ne sayde
In alle his lif, unto no manere wight.
He was a veray parfit gentil knight.
   But for to tellen you of his araie,
His hors was good, but he ne was not gaie.
Of fustian he wered a gipon,
Alle besmotred with his habergeon,
For he was late ycome from his viage,
And wente for to don his pilgrimage.[1]

You perceive at once the marks of Christianity.
Not by his fighting against the Turks, for that
was but the equivalent of Athenians fighting
against the barbarians of Thrace, or of Romans
against the Germans, but by "his port as is a
mayde," for the traditional gentleman, though
modest, was proud, and never much in love with
meekness and humility; also by his "besmotred
gipon," for the traditional gentleman made a great
point of appearance, and, even if he had just returned from traveling, would have appeared ready
for his pilgrimage, neat but not gaudy in costly
habit.

But let us go from fiction to history. Louis IX,
King of France, Saint Louis, was a great gentleman, and yet he erred, in our eyes at least, by
intemperance in his religion. He deemed it his
duty to sacrifice thousands of Frenchmen, giving

[1] Tyrwhitt's text.

[86]

them over to death, to wounds, to hunger, disease, and captivity, in order to establish certain theological dogmas and ecclesiastical rites in Jerusalem and the adjacent lands. Intemperance, as Antoninus Pius would have thought, in crusading, in asceticism, in religiosity, is a fault, but otherwise Saint Louis was a true gentleman; his life — what he did, what he said, what he was — is one of the *chefs-d'œuvre* in human conduct and, like the Van Eycks' picture "The Fountain of Life," or the twelfth-century windows in Chartres Cathedral, or Palestrina's *Libri missarum,* has become one of the heirlooms of our European heritage.

Saint Louis was a creature of privilege. Born of a line of kings, he was bred in a palace, educated by his queen mother, and moulded by those influences that constructed Notre-Dame-de-Paris, carved the statues of Rheims and Chartres, and colored the glass that still remains the best interpretation of the Christian hope. He was mightily courageous; four times, Joinville says, he voluntarily ran the hazard of his life. Once, off Cyprus, his ship, on board which there were eight hundred souls, ran aground and wrenched the keel so badly that the master mariners all insisted that the King must enter another ship. "What!" he said, "and leave these eight hundred men, to whom their lives are as dear as mine to me!" And he stayed with the ship. He was devoted to the public good. Once, when ill, thinking that he might die, he said to his eldest son: "My dear son [*beau fils*] I beg you to make your people love you, for truly I had rather have a Scot come from Scotland to rule the people well and justly, than that you should rule them ill." He was temperate in his appetite. Joinville says: "He was so moderate in eating that I never heard him ask for any dish, as many rich men do, but he ate whatever was set before him. He was restrained in speech, I never heard him speak ill of anybody. . . . He mixed water with his wine." Once the King asked Joinville if he wished to be respected in this world and go to heaven on his death; Joinville answered that he did. Thereupon the King said: "Refrain from consciously doing or saying anything, that if everybody came to know of it, you would not wish to avow it and say, 'I did this, I said that.'" And, as to dress, he used to say that a man should so clothe and arm himself that experienced men of the world would say that he had gone to excess, and that young men would say that he had done too little. The King himself always dressed simply.

Everyone remembers the conversation between Saint Louis and Joinville about leprosy: "The King once called me to him and said: 'I am going to ask you,' he said, 'which would you rather do, be a leper or commit a deadly sin?' I had never lied to him, so I said I had rather commit thirty deadly sins than be a leper . . . and he said, 'You speak like a fool and a madman; for you should know that no leprosy is as foul as deadly sin, for a soul in deadly sin is like the devil; and no leper can be so foul as he. . . . So I urge you as forcibly as I can, for love of God and of me, to prefer leprosy and every bodily ill than that death should enter into your soul.' " And at another time the King, being in high spirits, said to Joinville, "Sénéchal, give the reasons why a *prud'homme* [a man of honor] is better than a *béguin* [a sort of wandering beggar]." So Joinville and Maître Robert de Sorbon, the same that founded the famous Collège de la Sorbonne, set to arguing, and disputed for a long time. At last the King settled the controversy: "Maître Robert, I should very much like to take the name of *prud'homme*, supposing that I were one; and if I do, you may have all else that's left, for *prud'homme* is so great and so good a thing, that mere saying the word fills the mouth."

Not since Marcus Aurelius wore the Roman purple — of whom the Emperor Julian (he that Christians call "the Apostate") said that his soul was like a light shining through alabaster — has a monarch been so full of goodness and of charm. The points on which he fell away — differed, I mean — from the type of gentleman as accepted by the Greeks and Romans consisted in his excessive belief in Christian dogma, and in his lack of pride. On other points he would have satisfied the sternest standards, for you will remember that he asserted himself and his rights against Henry III of England, winning the Battle of Taillebourg, and also against the prelates of his realm, who sought to encroach upon the royal prerogatives on behalf of Rome. *Fortitudo, justitia,* he possessed in generous measure, and also *temperantia* and *prudentia,* except in this matter of fighting Saracens. He had taste, as you shall see, if you look beneath Viollet-le-Duc's restorations in the Sainte-Chapelle. His manners were charming. You may see the impression he left upon public opinion in the gracious figure painted by Giotto in the Bardi Chapel in Santa Croce, a memorial of military and political duty done, of manners, style, taste, modesty, of privacy, so far as his exigent mother, Blanche of Castile, would allow. As to the humanities, they fared ill in those days of theological domination.

Antoninus Pius, Alcibiades, Sarpedon, Lord Chesterfield, and George Wyndham, of whom I am to speak, would have loved to dine with him.

XIV

AT THE COURT OF URBINO (1507)

IN our days, hearkening to our political leaders
and to our preachers, we assume that equality
is an absolute good, and that whatever is detri-
mental to equality or inconsistent with it should
and will be swept away; so, somewhat in like
fashion, but contrariwise, earlier generations, as in
Italy about the time of the pontificates of Julius II
and Leo X, assumed, perhaps too readily, that
inequality was an immutable law of society, that
a nobility was an absolute good, and the Guild
of Gentlemen an invaluable social factor. Of all
writers on the qualifications for membership in
this Guild, Baldassare Castiglione is the most celebrated. Visitors to the Louvre know the quiet,
gentle, intelligent face, not untouched by resigna-
tion, in Raphael's portrait.

The principality of Urbino lent itself to appreciation of the Guild of Gentlemen, for it was
one of those delightful, fantastic little states that
one hardly expects to find outside of fairy tales.

Only the romantic Italy of the Renaissance could produce such a dukedom, a sort of miniature Utopia fit for Prospero and Miranda, but established and made famous by quite a different person, Federigo da Montefeltro, the masterful prince with the broken nose that Piero della Francesca painted for us. Federigo's son Guidubaldo succeeded to his father and married a distinguished lady, Elisabetta Gonzaga, of the ruling house of Mantua, sister to the husband of the celebrated Isabella d'Este, she who stands among the foremost women of her time, only yielding precedence to Isabella of Castile. At this little court of Urbino, centred about the Duchess Elisabetta, a group of gentlemen gathered together, who in the arts and graces of urbanity were the most accomplished in Europe. They lived in a happy time, at the crest of the great wave of exaltation that heaved the arts so high in Italy; and Castiglione chose, for reasons local to Urbino, the year 1507 as that of the discussion in the Duchess's salon, if I may use that term, concerning the qualifications for the Guild of Gentlemen, which he purports to recount in his book. At this time, Raphael was painting Madonnas; Giorgione and Titian were immortalizing less pious subjects; Michelangelo was modeling a tomb for Julius II; Leonardo planning, contriving, and prophetically imagining at Milan; Bramante was building the basilica of Saint Peter's; Machiavelli endeavoring to put some of his political ideas into practice by organizing a militia in Florence; Ariosto composing cantos of *Orlando Furioso;* Guicciardini still practising at the bar — in all respects the tide of luxury and enjoyment of the intellectual things of life was running high.

The Duchess Elisabetta Gonzaga was a cultivated, accomplished, and charming *grande dame* and, magnetlike, attracted connoisseurs in the art of manners about her — Ottaviano and Federigo Fregoso, two gentlemen of Genoa; Giuliano de' Medici, whose tomb by Michelangelo is one of the treasures of Florence; Pietro Bembo, a very distinguished humanist and future cardinal; Count Lodovico da Canossa, a friend of Raphael's; Gaspar Pallavicino, of a great Lombard family; Bernardo Bibbiena, a clever man of the world, a patron of Raphael and future cardinal; Francesco Maria della Rovere, grandnephew to Pope Julius II and future Duke of Urbino, and such. The company was accustomed to leisure and luxury; and, indeed, upon leisure and luxury depends the capacity, or at least the inclination, to consider manners as a fine art; but these gentlemen were far from being idlers, still farther from being wastrels, and their lives, like a lovely river — the

Dee, the Dordogne, or the Housatonic — flowing in predetermined banks, were in great measure directed and shaped by the social habits established at Urbino by Federigo da Montefeltro, him of the broken nose in Piero della Francesca's portrait, to whom I have alluded.

Vespasiano, a scholar who collected this Duke's library, says Federigo's "establishment at Urbino was conducted with the regularity of a religious fraternity, rather than that of a military household. Gambling and profanity were unknown, and a singular decorum of language was observed, whilst many noble youths, sent there to learn good manners and military discipline, were reared under the most exemplary tuition. He regarded his subjects as his children, and was at all times accessible to hear them personally state their petitions. . . . In summer he was in the saddle at dawn, and rode three or four miles into the country with half-a-dozen of his court. . . . When at table he listened to the Latin historians, chiefly Livy, except in Lent, when some religious book was read. . . . His fare was plain and substantial, denying himself sweet dishes and wine, except drinks of pomegranates, cherries, apples or other fruits. After dinner, or supper, an able judge of appeal stated in Latin the causes brought before him, and thereupon the Duke gave judgment in that language." You see that the tradition of the obligations attending privilege, as Sarpedon, as Antoninus Pius, as Saint Louis understood them, persisted, in complete integrity. Such a tradition, however strong, does not live of itself, but is dependent upon disciples that uphold and maintain it. The record of that discipleship at Urbino is contained in Castiglione's treatise, the *Book of the Courtier*, a treatise on what a gentleman should be.

The treatise, as I say, purports to record conversations that took place in the Duchess's apartments in the palace at Urbino. I shall not attempt to do more than indicate the notes of a gentleman, upon which Castiglione lays emphasis. The first requisite, though the rule gave way to the knocking of talent, was that a gentleman should not start at scratch, but with a handicap, at an advantage — he should be born in the patrician class. This was partly due to a belief in heredity, that children of parents of special endowments, or character, would more readily than others become such persons as, for example, Plato wished to be guardians in his republic, and, being inheritors of a tradition, would more gladly and faithfully guard it, would feel more pride in success, more shame in failure, than was possible for persons born outside of the tradition; but it was also partly due to the belief in environment (though that convenient word did not then lie ready to hand), in early education and association, in an early habit of giving commands and accepting obedience. As to the other traits, they were very much what I have indicated. The speakers differ in certain particulars, but in no essential point; as always, the fundamental qualities relate to military and political duties.

Great stress is laid on manners. The first speaker, Count Lodovico da Canossa, begins with a eulogy upon a gentleman eminent by birth and fortune, who is all grace and graciousness, charming in conversation, gesture, and looks, whether with high or low — in fact, a paragon of style in the art of human intercourse. Style in conduct, carried to this point, is a bridge between the accomplished gentleman of the world and the true Christian, since such manners testify to a solicitude for another's happiness, and that is for the nonce equivalent to the behavior of the Good Samaritan.

Modesty is insisted upon. A true gentleman, though foremost in the fight, in every other place will be modest and reserved. He will shun ostentation and all self-praise. He will avoid all affectation; and that is the surest means, in case nature has been niggard to him, of acquiring what grace may be possible. And in his insistence upon this theme, Count Lodovico uses an unusual word, *sprezzatura*, to designate "a concealment of art, making it appear, as it were, that whatever is said or done, is said or done without effort, as if unconsciously." Then he explains that this quality is more genuine and more subtle than that; that what he really means is that an accomplished gentleman will bestow careful thought upon his actions or words, but none upon the impression that those actions or words may make upon the bystanders. This *sprezzatura* is a charming quality, but rather the result of what a man is than an acquirable accomplishment, unless a man can make himself such that *sprezzatura* becomes part of his nature. The fundamental quality beneath it is a pure and lovable simplicity. You see that in some respects, as I said, the influence of Christianity has enhanced the charm of a gentleman's qualities.

The company discusses style in its relation to language at great length. A speaker or writer must first of all have something to say, and he should say it in well-marshaled sentences and in words that are precise, well chosen, and as far as possible in familiar use in ordinary life. The speaker's voice should be sonorous, clear, sweet, and under control. But, always, the ideas beneath the words are the important thing. You see that, in the opinion of Conte Baldassare Castiglione, the Guild of Gentlemen are the guardians of style in speech and writing.

Nothing specific is said about the humanities, using that word in the sense of Greek and Latin classics, but a good deal about general cultivation, the necessity of a knowledge of literature, of foreign languages, and of the fine arts. And there shall be, as a matter of course, great reverence for women; there shall also be a proper attention to dress; there shall be, also as a matter of course, athletic exercises — riding, hunting, and suchlike. But the fundamental element in a member of the Guild, according to the opinion prevalent in Urbino, is character, and character must manifest itself in outward behavior: a gentleman should be courteous, kind, generous, affable, and pleasant in society, dutiful and diligent in the performance of his duties, and he should seek to further the advantage and the honor of his friends, whether present or absent — putting up with their defects, never quarreling over unimportant matters, and seeking to correct faults in himself that friends may point out. And for a general precept, the gentleman follows the golden mean, behaves with a *certa onesta mediocrità*, both in word and in deed.

You see that I was quite right in my assertion

that Christianity enhanced the charm of the gentleman in certain respects, though its effects were deleterious in others, and also right in saying that all this delightful cultivation of that most important element in life, good manners, is dependent upon leisure and luxury, upon property and privilege. At least, it was so in Urbino in the time of Raphael, Michelangelo, and Leonardo.

XV

TEMPORE QUEEN ELIZABETH

THE reign of Queen Elizabeth, though Richard Hooker speaks of "this present age full of tongue and weak of brain," looks to us, as we see it in perspective, abounding in energy and accomplishment. Poets, pirates, dramatists, thinkers, — Sidney, Spenser, Shakespeare, Marlowe, Frobisher, Humphrey Gilbert, Drake, Raleigh, Bacon, Hooker, — rhyming, brawling, praying, raiding the Spanish Main, writing tumultuous poetry and majestic prose; all its world seems bursting, from the blossom to the full fruitage, with physical and mental vigor. And never, perhaps, in all English history, was the Guild of Gentlemen held in higher esteem. It was a warlike time, and war was well thought of. And, in the same general way as the heroes of Homeric times, as the guardians in Plato's *Republic*, gentlemen were primarily fighting men. Without *fortitudo*, an Elizabethan, no matter how high his birth, was no better than a churl, but a gentleman

had other indispensable qualities. Gentle a
gentleman should be, in manners, carriage, speech,
whether with his equals, his superiors, his inferiors,
whether with men or women. And in that generation, these qualities were recognized to confer
such benefits upon society, and were so highly
prized, that they were believed to be inherited,
to belong to certain families, to run with the blood,
so to speak.

Sir Philip Sidney

> . . . as he fought
> And as he fell . . .
> Sublimely mild, a Spirit without spot,

is usually taken as the paradigm. Fathers are
often just, and his father said: "He is a rare ornament of his age, the very formula that all well-
disposed young gentlemen of our court do form
also their manners and life by. In truth, I speak
it without flattery of him or myself, he hath the
most virtues that ever I found in any man. . . .
I say imitate him." For, although we often think
of him as occupying a certain place in English
literature, nevertheless, as Fulke Greville says,
"The truth is, his end was not writing, even while
he wrote; nor his knowledge moulded for tables
and schools; but both his wit and understanding
bent upon his heart, to make himself, and others,

not in words or opinion, but in life and action, good and great." And a hundred years later Sir William Temple — for the testimony of an alien generation is the best witness to truth — said that Sir Philip Sidney was "a person born capable not only of forming the greatest idea, but leaving the noblest example, if the length of his life had been equal to the excellence of his wit and his virtues."

And as Fulke Greville ascribes to him other qualities that belong to the ideal gentleman, I will quote him further: "A man fit for conquest, plantation, reformation, or what action soever is greatest and hardest amongst men: withal such a lover of mankind, and goodness, that whosoever had any real parts, in him found comfort, participation, and protection to the uttermost of his power. . . . The universities abroad, and at home, accounted him a general Mæcenas of learning . . . soldiers honored him . . . men of affairs in most parts of Christendom entertained correspondency with him . . . his heart and capacity were so large, that there was not a convincing painter, a skilful engineer, an excellent musician, or any other artificer of extraordinary fame, that made not himself known to this famous spirit, and found him a true friend without hire, and the common rendezvous of worth in his time . . . neither was this in him a private, but a public affection; his chief ends being, not friends, wife, children, and himself, but above all things the honour of his Maker, and the service of his prince or country."

Add to this that Sidney lived in castles and palaces, by birth a Dudley through his mother, and on his father's side "of ancient and always well-esteemed and well-matched gentry," a minion of privilege; he was (I quote again), "if ever there was one, a gentleman finished and complete, in whom mildness was associated with courage, erudition mollified by refinement, and courtliness dignified by birth. He is a specimen of what the English character was capable of producing. . . . The very stiffness it then possessed had a noble original; it was the natural consequence of that state of society, when the degrees of order and subordination were universally observed and understood, when the social relations were not broken down by the encroaching power of innovation, and where each was as ready to pay as to exact his tribute of observance and respect." So much for Sidney; and he, if ever a man was, is the achievement of privilege; and, as I say, the Elizabethan world held that such merchandise was worth the price.

But, Sidney apart, the mirror of the gentleman is framed in Shakespeare's plays. There, more than in any ideal republic or Utopia, gentlemen and ladies cross the stage, in cogent argument of the advantage to society of the Guild of Gentlemen. Unless one is prepared to deny that the goddesses from the pediment of the Parthenon, Michelangelo's "Pietà," Donatello's "Saint George," Verocchio's "Colleoni," are not worth the pains they cost; that the cathedrals of Chartres, Rheims, and Amiens are creations of perverted genius; that the Van Eycks, Mantegna, Piero della Francesca, Botticelli, Titian, Tintoretto, El Greco, Rembrandt, Watteau, Velásquez, that Bach, Beethoven, Brahms, Wagner, Verdi, Bizet, might have been better employed, one must grant that the social value of a gentleman, of a lady, was never more excellently demonstrated than by Shakespeare. Hamlet, not merely by what he says, but as we see him in the eyes of Ophelia, of the Queen, of Horatio, of Fortinbras, is indeed a glass of fashion and a mould of form for members of the Guild forever. And Othello, when he warns the brawlers, "Keep up your bright swords, for the dew will rust them," or when he woos Desdemona, or even in his death (for the self-restraints of gentle breeding burst like the flanks of Vesuvius before the rush of mad passion), is the great gentleman, and Brutus is another.

Or, clearer and more notable still, take the ladies: Cordelia, Ophelia, Brutus's Portia, Juliet,

— even Lady Macbeth, like though she be to Medusa, is a lady, — and the high-bred young heroines of the comedies, Beatrice, Rosalind, Viola, Miranda, Perdita. Never was queen or empress attended by such a company. They are all the works of privilege, of leisure and luxury, born to parents in high place; young, beautiful, waited upon by trained damsels; their paths smoothed, except for the exigencies of the plot; their clothes elegant, their manners polished, their speech delicate, their voices tunable. One might say that Shakespeare's great benefaction to mankind was to portray gentlemen and ladies. In future times posterity will read with astonishment of this strange breed of men, and perhaps — if democracy continues triumphant — sneer at a civilization which did not see that they were parasites, the offspring of inequality and injustice, always wronging such fine fellows as themselves.

XVI

THE COMPLEAT GENTLEMAN (1627)

BY Peacham's time, as well as in Queen Elizabeth's, the observed facts that children bred in the homes of well-mannered parents acquired not only their way of speech, their deportment, their singularities, but also their tastes, induced a belief that the attributes of the gentry were inherited; that a gentleman belonged to a species and, by the accident of birth, "reflected as from a fair glass, whatever princely moderation and honesty of heart, his ancestors might have possessed, and the honorably disposed mind, the love and admiration of whatever is honest or excellent, that marked his father." Peacham says: "As for the most part, wee see children of Noble Personages to beare the lineaments and resemblance of their Parents: so, in like manner, for the most part, they possess their virtues and Noble dispositions, which even in their tenderest yeares will bud forth, and discover it selfe." Nevertheless Peacham recognized that this was but a disposition, an aptitude, and needed to be cultivated, trained, and disciplined, and that oftentimes an innate nobility may entitle a man of mean birth to enter the Guild of Gentlemen. The estate of nobility, he says, is always open to merit, and noble stocks begin by conspicuous acts of public service, such as defeating the enemy in time of war, or by fortitude in civil matters, by greatness of spirit, by magnificence, by eloquence. But I must hurry on and merely quote what Peacham says concerning the notes that mark the Guild.

An essential part of nobility is learning, which for the culture of the mind is like a "conduit pipe whereby (as in a goodly garden) the sweet streames of heaven's blessings are conveyed in piety, peace, and plenty, to the nourishing of thousands, and the flourishing of the most ingenious arts and sciences." Learning, the equivalent of what I have spoken of as an education in the humanities, is insisted upon; it is a dignity — more than that, a necessity for gentlemen. There must be culture of the mind and correctness of manners. And in the matter of speaking and writing, Mr. Peacham insists upon style: "Labour first by all means to get the habit of a good stile in speaking and writing. I call with Tully that a good and eloquent stile of speaking, 'When there is a judicious fitting of choice words, apt and grave sentences unto matter well disposed, the same being uttered with a comely moderation of the voice, continuance and gesture.' . . . Let your stile therefor be furnished with solid matter, and compact of the best, choice and most familiar words." You see how closely he agrees with Baldassare Castiglione; both follow the Latin tradition. And he counsels young gentlemen to "make choice of those authors in prose, who speak the best and purest English." And he says, "To sweeten your severer studies, vouchsafe Poetry your respect," for she "holdeth so sovereigne a power over the minde, can turne brutishnesse into civility, make the lewd honest, turne hatred to love, cowardice into valour, and in briefe, like a Queene command overall affection."

The Compleat Gentleman, for it is such a one that Mr. Peacham has in mind, should be acquainted with music, at least if he have any natural disposition thereto, more for his pleasure and spiritual benefit, it would seem, than for his intellectual advantage, "since it is a principall meanes of glorifying our mercifull Creator, it heightens our devotion, it gives delight and ease to our traveler, it expelleth sadnesse and heavinesse of Spirit, preserveth people in concord and amity, allayeth fiercenesse, and anger; and lastly, is the best Phisicke for many melancholy diseases." A gentleman should also be well informed about statues, inscriptions, and coins. Of statues Mr. Peacham says, "It is not enough for an ingenuous Gentleman to behold these with a vulgar eye; but he must be able to distinguish them, and tell who and what they be." He approves also of drawing and painting, "it being a quality most commendable, and so many ways usefull to a Gentleman." Nor is it amiss to know something about the history of painting, or the lives of painters. "Since the Civill end of our life is, *ut in honore cum dignitate vivamus*, you shall withall find good learning and the Arts to conferre a great helpe and furtherance hereunto, being a polisher of un-bred rudenesse and our informity, and a curer of many diseases our minds are subject unto: for we learne not to begge to our selves admiration from other, or boastingly to lay to view so rich and precious furniture of our minds, but that wee may be useful to others, but first to ourselves."

A gentleman, too, should know about heraldry, the outward marks that custom had imposed to distinguish persons of quality from others. But more important is the exercise of the body, since "the mind from the ability of the Body gathers her strength and vigor." Riding, — which is especially necessary for men who shall be officers in the army, — running, jumping, swimming, shooting, hawking, and hunting, "for there is no one exercise that enableth the body more for the warre, than hunting, by teaching you to endure heate, cold, hunger, thirst; to rise early, watch late, lie and fare hardly." And he cites an example: "The old Lord Gray (our English Achilles) when hee was Deputie of Ireland, to inure his sonnes for the warre, would usually in the depth of Winter, in frost, snow, rain, and what weather soever fell, cause them at midnight to be raised out of their beds and carried abroad on hunting till the next morning; then perhaps come wet and cold home, having for a breakfast, a browne loafe and a mouldie cheese, or (which is ten times worse) a dish of Irish butter." And Mr. Peacham adds: "But as we allow not altogether that severe education of the old Spartans in their children, hazarding many times the healths of young and tender bodies, by some tedious ague; yea, also their lives, by the mischance of a leape or stumbling of a horse: so as much doe I detest that effœminancy of the most, that burne out day and night in their beds, and by the fireside; in trifles, gaming, or courting their yellow mistresses all the winter in a City; appearing but as Cuckoes in the spring, one time in the year to the Countrey and their tenants, leaving the care of keeping good houses at Christmas, to the honest Yeomen of the Country."

And remember that all this discipline of the mind and training of the body is for the sake of character and conduct, "without which our most graceful gifts are dead and dull." Character and conduct constitute "the Crowne of Good parts." The principal means to preserve this crown "is Temperance, and that Moderation of the mind, wherewith as a bridle we curbe and breake our ranke and unruly passions, keeping as the Caspian Sea, ourselves ever at one height without ebbe or refluxe. . . . For Moderation of the mind and affections, which is the Ground of all Honesty, I must give you that prime receipt . . . the feare of God, without which our judgments are depraved, and left to ourselves, we are not able to give anything his true esteeme and value."

In this desultory way Henry Peacham sets down what I have called the notes of a gentleman — readiness for service in war or politics, manners, style, taste, modesty, knowledge of the humanities, training of the body, observance of the cardinal virtues, and so forth. And now I will show the result of such training, the summing up of these accompaniments and derivatives of privilege in Lord Clarendon's portrait of Falkland: —

A person of such prodigious parts of learning and knowledge, of that inimitable sweetness and delight in conversation, of so flowing and obliging a humanity and goodness to mankind, and of that primitive simplicity and integrity of life, that if there were no other brand upon this odious and accursed civil war [The Great Rebellion] than that single loss, it must be most infamous, and execrable to all posterity. . . . Before this Parliament, his condition of life was so happy that it was hardly capable of improvement. Before he came to twenty years of age he was master of a noble fortune, which descended to him by the gift of a grandfather. . . . His education for some years had been in Ireland, where his father was Lord Deputy; so that when he returned into England to the possession of his fortune, he was unentangled with any acquaintance or friends, which usually grow up by the custom of conversation, and therefore was to make a pure election of his company, which he chose by other rules than were prescribed to the young nobility of that time. And it cannot be denied, though he admitted some few to his friendship for the agreeableness of their natures and their undoubted affection to him, that his familiarity and friendship for the most part was with men of the most eminent and sublime parts, and of untouched reputation in point of integrity; and such men had a title to his bosom.

He was a great cherisher of wit and fancy and good parts in any man; and, if he found them clouded with poverty or want, a most liberal and bountiful patron towards them, even above his fortune; of which in those administrations he was such a dispenser as if he had been trusted with it to such uses, and if there had been the least of vice in his expense, he might have been thought too prodigal. He was constant and pertinacious in whatever he resolved to do, and not to be wearied by any pains that were necessary to that end. And therefore, having once resolved not to see London (which he loved above all places) till he had perfectly learned the Greek tongue, he went to his own house in the country, and pursued it with that indefatigable industry that it will not be believed in how short a time he was master of it, and accurately read all the Greek historians.

In his time, his house being within little more than ten miles of Oxford, he contracted familiarity and friendship with the most polite and accurate men of that university; who found such an immenseness of wit, and such a solidity of judgment in him, so infinite a fancy bound in by a most logical ratiocination, such a vast knowledge that he was not ignorant in any thing, yet such an excessive humility as if he had known nothing, that they frequently resorted and dwelt with him, as in a college situated in a purer air; so that his house was a university bound in a lesser volume, whither they came not so much for repose as study, and to examine and refine those grosser propositions which laziness and consent made current in vulgar conversation. . . .

He was superior to all those passions and affections which attend vulgar minds, and was guilty of no other ambition than of knowledge, and to be reputed a lover of all good men; and that made him too much a contemner of those arts, which must be indulged in the transactions of human affairs. . . . And indeed he was so exact and strict an observer of justice and truth, *ad amussim,* that he believed those necessary condescensions and applications to the weakness of other men, and those arts and insinuations which are necessary for discoveries, and preventions of ill, would be in him a declension from the rule which he acknowledged fit and absolutely necessary to be practised in those employments; and was so precise in the practick principles he prescribed himself (to all others he was as indulgent), as if he had lived *in republica Platonis.* . . .

Such was this product of privilege.

Imagine, if you please, the company of unborn souls pressing about the gates of life, awaiting their turn. And one of them, an orator, a democrat, a Unitarian clergyman, perchance, proposes that all agree that they shall share and share alike in natural endowments of body and mind, in beauty, in quickness of wit, in grace and elegance, and also in all the gifts of fortune, in the rank and virtue of parents, in property, in climate, in scenery, and so forth, and that all shall be alike as peas. Suppose, also, that another unborn orator arose, and made a contrary suggestion that all such good things of nature and fortune be heaped together and divided into separate heaps — one a sort of jack pot, and little heaps, and lesser heaps, and emptinesses, all corresponding to lottery tickets, some carrying a prize of this value, another of that, others quite blank, and one that bore away the jack pot. Do you not believe that *le bon Dieu* has been kind enough to endow these unborn souls with sporting spirit, and that the majority of those who prefer a lottery over those who want equal pay envelopes would be overwhelming? From all — but that is not much — that I have been able to learn of *le bon Dieu*, inequality is his favorite hobby.

XVII

THE REIGN OF QUEEN ANNE

HISTORY had moved on. The Restoration did not accept in its fullness the theory that ethics constitute a necessary element in the making of a gentleman. The current conception laid stress on a gentleman's privileges, on his elegance, on his observance of etiquette, on his right to leisure and pleasure, and prepared the way for a widespread general skepticism as to the social value of such a gentleman. The stage of the period usually depicts him as a rake and a fop, "buckling shoes, gartering, combing and powdering," a creature of bravado and brag, of idleness, gallantry, and impertinent disrespect to persons of inferior station, until, even taking into account the theatrical habit of comic exaggeration, it is hard not to believe that there is truth in the picture.

Sir Harry Wildair (I quote from Farquhar's comedy of that name), who is both gay and brave, is a fair portrait: "He's a gentleman of

most happy circumstances, born to a plentiful estate; has had a genteel and easy education, free
from the rigidness of teachers and pedantry of
schools. His florid constitution being never ruf-
fled by misfortune, nor stinted in its pleasures, has
rendered him entertaining to others, and easy to
himself: — turning all passion into gaiety of humor." Not a bad fellow, but no great contribution to society. Lord Foppington in *The Relapse*
(Vanbrugh) is of course a comic character, but
the likeness gave the part its piquancy. The town
gallant was a fop. The country gentleman was a
lout, and yet a lout with various good qualities.
Macaulay describes him as of the time of the
Restoration, with "his chief pleasures derived
from field sports and from an unrefined sensual-
ity," and his mind a confused mass of prejudices.
And yet the historian adds, "Unlettered as he was
and unpolished, he was still in some most important points a gentleman. He was a member of
a proud and powerful aristocracy. His family
pride was beyond that of a Talbot or a Howard.
He knew the genealogies and coats of arms of all
his neighbors . . . he was a magistrate, and as
such, administered gratuitously to those who dwelt
around him a rude patriarchal justice, which in
spite of innumerable blunders and of occasional
acts of tyranny, was yet better than no justice at

all. He was an officer of the trainbands. . . . His ignorance and uncouthness, his low tastes and gross phrases, would, in our time, be considered as indicating a nature and a breeding thoroughly plebeian. Yet he was essentially a patrician, and had, in large measure, both the virtues and the vices which flourish among men set from their birth in high place, and used to respect themselves and to be respected by others."

These pictures of the town gallant and the country gentleman show a large falling off from Shakespeare's gentlemen, from Sidney or Falkland. The gentleman lout of the Restoration, in his boorishness, and the gentleman fop in his excesses of etiquette, both agreed and united in a total abandonment of Aristotle's mean. But these types did not last long; by the time of Queen Anne's reign, the reaction from the Puritan régime had spent itself, and the traditional social uses of the gentleman were again insisted upon — good breeding, benevolence, the cultivation of non-utilitarian interests, the embellishment of leisure. Mr. Darell, in his book, *The Gentleman Instructed* (1723), shows an unquestioning confidence in the institution of the Guild of Gentlemen: —

Some Gentlemen keep up to their character without the advantageous Helps of Precepts, or Education; you may read their Birth on their Faces; their Gate and Mein tell their Quality; they both Charm and Awe, and at the same time flash Love and Reverence; their Extraction glitters under all Disguises; it sparkles in Sackcloth, and breaks through all the Clouds of Poverty and Misfortune; there is a *je ne sçay quoy* in their whole Demeanour, that tears off the Vizor, and discovers Nobility, though it sculks *incognito*; they are reserved without Pride, and familiar without Meanness; they time their Behaviour to Circumstances, and know when to stand on Tip-toe, and when to stop: In fine, their most trivial Actions are Great and their Discourse is Noble.

There are, the author admits, in agreement with the dramatists that I quoted, so-called gentlemen of quite a different caste, "Clown without and Coxcomb within," and in between these two categories he says there are intermediate gentlemen, "who must acquire Behaviour like any other Art, by Study and Application." Gentlemen avoid gross language and oaths. They do not boast; they observe the niceties of breeding, they carry their principles into social life and do not "lay them at the Door with their Goloshoes." They improve their time by "the handsome Diversion" of reading, and cultivate their minds, and their conversation is in marked contrast to those whose "Discourse is a compound of Smut and Rallery, enlivened always with Fooleries, and

sometimes seasoned with Oaths and Blasphemies."
They fight shy of too close communion with those
greater than themselves, and also with those below them; they will not herd with peasants, for
"Peasantry is a disease." They manage their
estates with prudence, are neither covetous nor
profuse, and live with an elegance suited to their
means. They hunt and hawk and practise all
manly sports, they dance and interest themselves
in music, "for when Reason runs low and Conversation languishes, a Stroke of the Fiddle, a
Song or a *Saraband* well performed may enliven
it," but these accomplishments do not touch the
essence of a gentleman, "they only fit him for a
modish Address and a Female entertainment."
As to dress they follow Polonius' advice. "They
are neat without Gaudiness, Genteel without Affectation."

Here, you see, the class of gentlemen is accepted
as part of the order of society, at best as an ornament, and there is scant attention to the theory
that a privileged class must justify itself by its
service to society as a whole.

But the stage at which the evolution of a gentleman had arrived in Queen Anne's time is best
set forth in Steele's description of Sir Roger de
Coverley: —

THE REIGN OF QUEEN ANNE

The first of our Society is a Gentleman of Worcester-shire, of antient Descent, a Baronet, his Name Sir Roger de Coverley. His great Grandfather was Inventor of that famous Country-Dance which is call'd after him. All who know that Shire are very well acquainted with the Parts and Merits of Sir Roger. He is a Gentleman that is very singular in his Behaviour, but his Singularities proceed from his good Sense, and are Contradictions to the Manners of the World, only he thinks the World is in the wrong. However, this Humour creates him no Enemies, for he does nothing with Sourness or Obstinacy; and his being unconfined to Modes and Forms, makes him but the readier and more capable to please and oblige all who know him. When he is in town he lives in Soho-Square. It is said, he keeps himself a Bachelor by reason he was crossed in Love, by a perverse beautiful widow of the next County to him. Before this Dis-appointment, Sir Roger was what you call a fine Gentle-man, had often supped with my Lord Rochester and Sir George Etherege, fought a Duel upon his first coming to Town, and kick'd Bully Dawson in a publick Coffee-house for calling him Youngster. But being ill used by the above-mentioned Widow, he was very serious for a Year and a half; and though, his Temper being naturally jovial, he at last got over it, he grew careless of himself, and never dressed afterward; he continues to wear a Coat and Doublet of the same Cut that were in Fashion at the Time of his Repulse, which, in his merry Humours, he tells us, has been in and out twelve Times since he first wore it. 'T is said Sir Roger grew humble in his Desires after he had forgot this cruel Beauty, insomuch that it is reported he has frequently offended in Point of Chastity with Beggars and Gypsies; but this is looked upon by his Friends rather as Matter of Raillery than Truth. He is now in his Fifty Sixth year, cheerful, gay and hearty, keeps a good house in Town and Country; a great Lover of Mankind; but there is such a mirthful cast in his Behaviour, that he is rather beloved than esteemed; His Tenants grow rich, his servants look satisfied, all the Young Women profess Love to him, and the Young Men are glad of his Company; When he comes into a House he calls the Servants by their names, and talks all the way up Stairs to a Visit. I must not omit that Sir Roger is Justice of the Quorum; that he fills the chair at a Quarter-Session with great Abilities, and three months ago gain'd universal Applause by explaining a Passage in the Game-Act.

Sir Roger is an agreeable type, but he is in nowise a fair representative of the Guild of Gentlemen as it was understood to be in the other epochs to which I refer. He does his political duties as a country magistrate, and no doubt would have been ready to fight and die for England, and his manners were in their way charming; but of style, of the humanities, he possessed nothing, and no love of privacy, no resemblance to Antoninus Pius, Saint Louis, or Sir Philip Sidney, and yet Sir

Roger is the best of the characters that one finds in the literature of the time. The reason for this falling off is due, as I think, to the political and religious perturbations in England. The Protestant Reformation had dealt a hard blow at the great social institution of tradition, at the unity of Christendom, at the Church, at monarchy, and at aristocracy. Calvinism in especial tended towards democracy, towards social leveling, towards disrespect for the past. And in England the Puritans hit the traditional type of gentleman hard; they beheaded the king, they overturned the Anglican Church, and with these two institutions, Monarchy and Church, the fortunes of the Guild of Gentlemen were closely bound. The effect of these perturbations appears in Sir Harry Wildair, Lord Foppington, and the general dislocation of the traditional type. It required another generation or two for the type to readjust itself to changed conditions, and again render itself of notable advantage to society.

XVIII

LORD CHESTERFIELD

THE preceding chapters show that the ideal of a gentleman does not correspond with the Christian ideal, — the ideal which asserted that Christ was the first true gentleman, — nor with the Epicurean ideal, which counseled the pursuit of the greatest sum of satisfactions and turned its back on war and politics, nor with the Stoical ideal, which disregarded the æsthetic side of life, made little of manners, of taste, and such matters. The Guild of Gentlemen postulated service in war, and, in time of peace, cultivation of the arts, of the humanities; it set store by manners, style, modesty, taste, privacy, and class education; but, as we have seen, different epochs, different generations, laid stress now on one of those qualities, now on another. In Homeric times stress was laid upon war; in the time of Pericles upon war, taste, æsthetics; under the Antonines, on the cardinal virtues; in the thirteenth century on *fortitudo, justitia,* and the mellowing influences shed upon conduct by Christianity; in Elizabethan times, upon intellect, high romance, manners, and style, as Shakespeare, Spenser, Bacon, Raleigh, and Hooker show. The ideal was always affected by the dominant character of the epoch. Profligacy dominated under the Restoration, quiet gentility in the time of Queen Anne. But the fundamental assumptions of property and privilege of leisure and luxury remain constant, and the notes of a gentleman that I enumerated in Part One are never lost sight of, though now one and then another stands out in high relief. I have now to refer to an eighteenth-century type best represented by the celebrated Lord Chesterfield, more especially because the type has been unfairly treated.

Lord Chesterfield, I say, has been treated with gross unfairness by common report, and in this report, perhaps, we can detect the first open stirrings of democratic opposition to the Guild of Gentleman. Common report seized upon an epigram made against Lord Chesterfield by Dr. Johnson, an epigram that to the democratic mind gained greatly in pungency because Dr. Johnson was a stout upholder of tradition. You remember his pronouncement when somebody suggested that a rich merchant might well be admitted to the Guild. "There may be some, he said, who think that a new system of gentility might be established, upon principles totally different from what have hitherto prevailed. Our present heraldry, it may be said, is suited to the barbarous times in which it had its origin. It is chiefly founded upon ferocious merit, upon military excellence. Why in civilized times, we may be asked, should there not be rank and honor, upon principles, which, independent of long custom, are certainly not less worthy, and which, when once allowed to be connected with elevation and precedency, would obtain the same dignity in our imagination? Why should not the knowledge, the skill, the expertness, the assiduity, and the spirited hazards of trade and commerce, when crowned with success, be entitled to give those flattering distinctions by which mankind are so universally captivated? Such are the specious, but false, arguments for a proposition which always will find numerous advocates, in a nation where men are every day starting up from obscurity to wealth. To refute them is needless. The general sense of mankind cries out with irresistible force, *'Un Gentilhomme est toujours Gentilhomme.'* "

Coming from Dr. Johnson, then, the epigram that Lord Chesterfield's *Letters to His Son* "teach

the morals of a whore, and the manners of a danc-
ing master," sounds very damaging to the importance attached by the Guild of Gentlemen to outward deportment, to behavior, to manners. But,
on the contrary, if one looks closer at Lord Chesterfield, one will take away a sense that he is a very
strong witness in favor of the advantage of the
Guild to society. In the first place his politeness
was such that his name has passed into the language
as a synonym for excellence of manners, and his
conversation was equal to his politeness, and there
was no element of what we call snobbery in him.
"Birth goes for nothing with me," he said; and,
"I used to think myself in company as much above
me when in company with Mr. Addison and Mr.
Pope, as if I had been with all the princes in Europe." Johnson himself admitted "the enchant-
ment of his address." And, unless one has a
strong democratic conviction of the superiority of
the absence of good manners, one is apt to think,
as age comes on and one looks back and reckons
up the credits and debits in the ledger of happiness, that the good manners of family, of friends,
of acquaintance, of strangers, make an accumulation of little emotions of inward warmth that
amount to a very considerable item on the credit
side.

So much for Lord Chesterfield's contribution

to the casual pleasure of chance meetings. In the fundamental matter of public service, he was equally laudable. All historians are agreed upon his success as Viceroy to Ireland. Lecky says: "The Viceroyalty of Chesterfield, though it unfortunately only lasted for eight months, was eminently successful. He came over in the beginning of the rebellion, 1745 [in Scotland], and the care with which he watched over the material prosperity of the country, the happy ridicule with which he discouraged the rumours of Popish risings, the firmness with which he refused to follow the precedent of 1715, when all Catholic chapels were closed during the rebellion, the unusual public spirit with which he administered his patronage, and the tact he invariably exhibited during the very critical circumstances of the times, made his government one of the most remarkable in Irish history." As to Lord Chesterfield's interest in the fine arts and the humanities, it may be said that he filled his villa at Blackheath with pictures, that he was well read in French literature, and kept up his Latin. But it is to his advice to the next generation that we must go in order to learn his opinion of the qualities necessary in a member of the Guild of Gentlemen. I quote from his letters to his young kinsman and godson, Philip Stanhope, a lad at school: —

LORD CHESTERFIELD

DEAR PHIL, I cannot enough inculcate into you, the absolute necessity, and infinite advantages of pleasing, that is *d'être aimable;* and . . . the first great step towards pleasing, is to desire to please. . . . The lowest and the poorest people in the world, expect good breeding from a gentleman, and they have a right to it; for they are by nature your equals, and are no otherwise your inferiors than by their education and their fortune. . . . You will ask me perhaps what you must do to be *aimable?* Do but resolve to be so, and the business is almost done. . . . Remember that there is no one thing so necessary for a gentleman as to be perfectly civil and well-bred. . . . Les grâces du corps préviendront ceux qui ne vous connaissent pas d'ailleurs en votre faveur. Souvenez-vous qu'il ne faut négliger aucun des moyens de plaire, c'est le grand article dans le commerce du monde. Tâchez de plaire, par votre air, par vos manières, par vos mœurs, par votre douceur. [You see he gives a lesson in French as well as in manners to the boy.] . . . Les mœurs veulent dire une certaine *décence,* un *decorum,* une *bienséance,* dans la conduite, et en tout ce qu'on fait, et en tout ce qu'on dit dans le commerce ordinaire du monde. Par exemple, un homme qui a des mœurs, ne jure pas, ne s'enivre pas, ne joue pas, et ne donne aucun sujet de scandale. . . . En un mot il faut être parfaitement *honnête homme.* . . . Ce mot comprend bien des choses. . . . C'est ce que nous appelons *a gentleman,* c'est-à-dire un homme qui a de bonnes mœurs, des manières très polies, douces et nobles, et qui sait se bien conduire en toute compagnie, vis-à-vis d'un

IN PRAISE OF GENTLEMEN

chacun.[1] . . . Honnête en français, veut dire en Anglais *a gentleman, a very well-bred man, who behaves properly and politely in all companies. It is necessary that he should have an unblemished character into the bargain.* . . . Nobilitas sola est, et unica Virtus.

Whenever you present yourself, or are presented for the first time in company, study to make the first impression you give of yourself as advantageous as possible. This you can only do at first by what solid people commonly call trifles, which are *air, dress,* and *address.* Here, invoke the assistance of the Graces. Even that silly article of dress is no trifle upon these occasions. Never be the first nor the last in the fashion. Wear as fine clothes as those of your rank commonly do, and rather better than worse. . . . A young man especially at his first entrance into the world is generally judged by the company he keeps, and it is a very fair way of judging. . . . Good company consists of a number of people of a certain fashion (I do not mean birth) where the majority are reckoned to be people of sense and decent character, in short, of those who are universally allowed

[1] "A graceful deportment inclines those who know nothing else of you in your favor. Remember not to neglect any means of pleasing; that is the important thing in social life. Try to please, by your bearing, by your manners, by your amiability, by your behavior. By behavior I mean a certain propriety and decorum, a knowledge of the conventions, that show themselves in all that is said or done in good society. For instance, a man of good behavior does not swear, or get drunk, or gamble, or do anything to cause scandal. . . . In short, you must be in every sense an *honnête homme.* That word comprises many things. It is what we call a gentleman in English, that is to say a man of good behavior, well-bred, amiable, high-minded, who knows how to act in any society, in the company of any man."

to be, and are called, good company. . . . Bear this
truth always in your mind, that you may be admired
for your wit if you have any, but that nothing but good
sense and good qualitys can make you be loved. . . .
You know how essential strict honor is to the character
of a Gentleman, as well as to the quiet of his mind, and
I am persuaded that you will never forget it; but if
upon any occasion you ever should, you will be the un-
happiest man in the world. . . . Il est certain qu'il
n'y a pour l'homme qu'un veritable malheur, qui est de
se trouver en faute, et d'avoir quelque chose à se re-
procher. Ayez toujours cette verité fixée dans votre
esprit. . . . Good breeding and a certain *suavitas
morum* shines and charms in every situation of life, with
relation to all sorts and ranks of people, as well the lowest as the highest. . . . You cannot conceive how
much that suavity of manners will endear you to everybody, even to those who have it not themselves. In high
life there are a thousand *minucies* of good breeding,
which though *minucies* in themselves, are so necessary
and agreeable, as to deserve your utmost attention and
imitation. As for instance what the French call *le bon
ton* or *le ton de la bonne compagnie*, by which is meant
the fashionable tone of good company. This consists
of many trifling articles in themselves, which when cast
up and added together, make a total of infinite consequence.

All this importance attached to the minutiæ
of conduct seems to the rugged democrat as so
much folderol. He has no taste for such matters,

he has no time to spend over trifles himself, and would prefer not to have other people waste their time over them. He is welcome to his opinion, and his opinion commends itself to the great majority of his fellow Americans; but I want to make it clear that these minutiæ are not, in Lord Chesterfield's judgment, to be severed from the serious virtues. He says: "A *gentleman* is a complex term, answers exactly to the French word *Honnête homme,* and comprehends manners, Decorum, Politeness, but above all strict Veracity; for without that all the accomplishments in the world avail nothing."

It is not that the polished gentleman of the eighteenth century cared less for what the democrat of to-day calls the solid virtues, but that in reckoning up the values of life, balancing good against ill, he found that the scale was often turned in favor of good, in favor of the worthwhileness of life, by an habitual giving and receiving of these little elegancies. And I cannot do better, in order to sum up this exposition of all aspects of a gentleman, than by quoting Lord Chesterfield once more: —

MY DEAR BOY, I dare say you have heard and read of the *Je ne sçay quoy,* both in French and English, for the expression is now adopted into our language; but I question whether you have any clear idea of it, and indeed it is more easily felt than deffined. It is a most estimable quality, and adorns every other. I will endeavor to give you a general notion of it, though I cannot an exact one; experience must teach it you, and will, if you attend to it. It is in my opinion a compound of all the agreeable qualitys of body and mind, in which no one of them predominates in such a manner as to give exclusion to any other. It is not mere wit, mere beauty, mere learning, nor indeed mere any one thing that produces it, though they all contribute something towards it. It is owing to this *Je ne sçay quoy* that one takes a liking to some one particular person at first rather than to another. One feels oneself prepossessed in favour of that person without being enough acquainted with him to judge of his intrinsick merit or talents, and one finds oneself inclined to suppose him to have good sense, good nature, and good humour. A genteel address, graceful motions, a pleasing elocution, and elegancy of style, are powerful ingredients in the compound. It is in short an extract of all the Graces. Here you will perhaps ask me to define the Graces, which I can only do by the *Je ne sçay quoy*, as I can only define the *Je ne sçay quoy* by the Graces. No one possesses them all, but happy he who possesses the most, and wretched he who possesses none of them. . . . Do not take into your head that these things are trifles; though they may seem so if singly and separately considered, yet when considered aggregately and relatively to the great and necessary art of pleasing, they are of infinite consequence.

IN PRAISE OF GENTLEMEN

Lord Chesterfield has much to say to his god-son about the necessity of "understanding Greek and Latin as well as a professor, and of knowing modern languages and history perfectly," but I confine myself here to the point of manners, for that is the note of a gentleman most obnoxious to a democracy and soonest disregarded.

XIX

GEORGE WYNDHAM

THE type persisted in England with greater stubbornness than in the United States, for the English social structure was far more thoroughly permeated by tradition, and though political democracy there has advanced fast and economic democracy is gaining ground, social democracy progressed but lamely until the Great War; and in the history of the latter part of the nineteenth century you will find the type as perfect as ever it was. I shall take George Wyndham as evidence to confirm my statement; in him you will find all the notes of the traditional gentleman — military service, political service, love of literature, receptivity to beauty, fine manners, style, modesty. He was born of privilege, bred upon privilege, enjoyed privilege all his life, and rendered full payment to society for all that he had received. I must dwell a little upon the luxury that surrounded him. In his first years he was often at his grandfather's place. "The great house with its treasures of art, the stables and the immense park with the South

Downs for background, made a romantic setting for the life of the nurseries." A little later his family established themselves at Cockermouth on the Derwent, "fairest of all rivers," and there Wyndham's mother used to read to her children Malory's *Morte d'Arthur*. Tradition nursed him on her knee, and romance entered into his childish games. It was a handsome family, and picture-loving visitors to the Metropolitan Museum seldom fail to see Sargent's portrait (said to have been painted in emulation of Sir Joshua Reynolds's "Three Graces") of Wyndham's beautiful sisters in all their aristocratic elegance and loveliness.

The first note of the traditional gentleman is readiness to take his stand, as Sarpedon said, in the front rank of the soldiers and encounter fiery battle. At twenty-one George Wyndham joined the Coldstream Guards, and the next year his battalion was ordered to Egypt. I will quote his father's letter to the young man as he embarked, for it helps one to understand the power and persistence of the patrician heritage: —

44 Belgrave Square, S.W.
February 19*th*, 1885

My Own Dearest, Dearest Boy.

I must say once how deeply I love you. I cannot express how I feel that my whole being is filled with *eager, tender love for you.* One cannot say this speaking, but I should never forgive myself if I had not told you. I know you feel all you give up in going away, but these occasions lift one up above all the petty accidents of Time and Space and leave Love and Duty standing as they will *stand forever.* This is what I mean when I say sometimes, "After all, nothing matters"; the dust in front of our own front door is all we are responsible for. This is a blessed thought. You know *how* I disapprove of the whole Egyptian business, so I like to tell you that I send you, my own dear boy, away quite as willingly as for the justest and most necessary war imaginable. I like you to know that I don't think *for a moment* your most *precious* life thrown away, if the worst comes, for sweet Duty's sake. We suffer for the sins and mistakes of others, as others in turn (dreadful thought) suffer and will suffer for ours, but judicially we are only responsible for what we do or leave undone ourselves. . . . God and all good Spirits keep you, my darling boy. I cannot make you know what I think of you, but I feel to have had such a son is not to have lived in vain. . . .

Ever your devoted Father
PERCY WYNDHAM

From the traditional military duty to the traditional political duty, George Wyndham proceeded in due course; secretary to Balfour, he entered Parliament, became Under-secretary for Foreign Affairs and Chief Secretary for Ireland. As for his duty of receptivity, — appreciation of the arts and public confession of their value, — his introductions to North's *Plutarch* and to *Shakespeare's Poems,* and his essays on "Ronsard" and on the "Springs of Romance in Literature," and his preface to Francis Thompson's *Shelley* are amplest proof. Again and again in his letters his love of literature crops out: "Occasionally I write verse again, and I read nothing except Vergil, Catullus, Shakespeare, Walter Scott and Boccaccio." And he set a high value on literary style. "Style," he said, "gives charm, surprise and color, but its greatest gift is beauty . . . all the masters of style have found the dodge of saying exactly what they mean in the fewest words." He had a great admiration for "the strength and grace and reticence of Greece and Rome." As to manners, he was as perfect as is possible. One of his Irish opponents, when he held office in Ireland, said: "Thank God, we have a gentleman as Chief Secretary." As for bodily exercises, — for they have always been demanded of patricians, — he was a great horseman, and devoted to fox hunting. At forty he writes: "It is jolly to find that twenty years cannot abate one's huge delight in riding to hounds." He was also devoted to the pleasures of privacy: "I dash to *Clouds* whenever I can and spend happy hours listening to the birds and arranging my books." He was the best-dressed man in the House of Commons, and he believed in gathering roses along the road of life: "What we need," he said, "is to have more feasting, song and flowers and wine, and sit long and late with beautiful ladies, ourselves crowned with wreaths," and to give you an idea of what a well-rounded person he was I will quote a letter written shortly before his death, in which he describes a dinner *al fresco* in France.

HOTEL LOTTI
7 ET 9 RUE DE CASTIGLIONE
PARIS, *4th June*, 1913

To Hilaire Belloc

. . . But — I would not for the world have missed the dinner I ate and the wine I drank at *Ledoyen:* Potage St. Germain. A Barbue — the whole of him with a sauce that was Maître d'Hôtel sublimated with mushrooms. A cold quail, stuffed with truffles and garnished with aspic and parsley, and supported by a salad. Hot Asperges vertes, as big as the white ones, with sauce mousseline. A cold salade Russe — without ham — but with a perfect mayonnaise. And then the best strawberries I can remember. For wine a Richebourg of 1890 which stood to other wines — and stands — in the relation of Homer and Shakespeare to other poets. It was a miracle of the Earth's entrails searched by the sun and responding with all the ethereal perfumes of a hot day in Summer tempered by the whispering and cool shadows of a breeze. No Jew was there. No American. No Englishman but myself. The French were dining under a sapphire sky, by an old willow-tree, a fountain and nymph in bronze. I had struck an oasis of civilization. There were few women, and that was fit. For how few women understand.

The service was traditional. One man — human and experienced — took the order and *reminded me* that I had forgotten the Asparagus. Another man — human and zealous — set the meats before me. Both rejoiced in my content and took their tips in the spirit of gentlemen knighted on the field of battle.

Such was George Wyndham, and in old times one such life would have been judged worth almost any price.

XX

ON PICTURESQUENESS

I HAVE now presented what I may call the reputation of a gentleman through the ages, what people thought gentlemen were and what they ought to be, so that we are now in a better position to weigh with even hand the benefits and the advantages to society at large from the institution. In other chapters I shall proceed to set forth the alien forces, to which I referred in the beginning, that have swept, or are sweeping, the Guild away. But those forces, it seems to me, have acted unconsciously more than consciously, and therefore the abolition of the Guild does not necessarily imply a formal condemnation of the Guild by the people, although I have no doubt that a universal vote would show an overwhelming majority against it, far greater in proportion than the majority which condemned Socrates. But before I take up the alien forces, let me refer to one aspect, the picturesque aspect, of the institution, as an argument, though of no great weight, in its favor.

Man is at bottom a theatrical animal; he likes drama, melodrama, he likes a variety show. Now, democracy is given over to the theory of equality, and equality implies sameness: it levels the hills, it builds its houses in town, its cottages in the country, so alike that often you can only distinguish them by painted numbers; it clothes men in ready-to-wear garments made wholesale, and would do the same with women were it not for their recalcitrant love of finery. That which makes the charm of tramping in England, or of motoring in France, is that in those countries the handiwork of man is of all sorts and kinds; there is a castle here, a cathedral there, a walled town, a village, a winding road, a straight avenue, poplar-lined, a park, a garden, a vineyard, a field, all indicative not merely of nature's abhorrence of equality, but indicative also of social inequality. Hundreds of visitors walk in uncomfortable groups through the multitudinous rooms of the Escurial, of Fontainebleau, of the Château de Chambord, day after day, because of the interest to see how the great used to live. Who strolls about Bath, or Rouen, or Bologna, or Rothenburg, and wishes for parallel streets of municipal three-story houses? Who, in front of the Minster of York, is vexed to find that the Anglican establishment is housed in one way and the nonconformist sects in another; or, at Troyes, because there are striking differences among the beautiful churches there? The natural man delights in differences, in contrasts, in the picturesque; he likes many colors, light and shade, shiftings, commotions, contraries. This is why everybody frequents the cinematograph. Who would go to a picture gallery if all the pictures were the same? Who to the Vatican if the statues were all alike? Who to a concert if the same piece were played over and over again?

One reason, then, that the destructive forces, with which I shall deal in the following chapters, have been withstood so long lies in this human fondness for the picturesque. The immense popularity of the *Waverley Novels* was due to the pageant of rank and class, of privilege and prerogative, of kings, crusaders, friars, lords, ladies, knights, squires, Jews, serfs, Highlanders, outlaws, and so forth. The *Canterbury Tales* have their great place in literature because the pilgrims are all brilliantly diverse in occupations, dress, and character. Kipling's fame is due to his pictured pages; Shaw delights us because of his unexpectednesses. Uniformity is the mother of boredom. The greatest praise bestowed upon Cleopatra was not for her beauty but for her "infinite variety."

And beside being a theatrical animal, man by nature likes to look up. He may possess this trait of looking up in a religious sense, and in the contemplation of things divine experience a thrill of awe and reverence; and this, where professional atheists do not interfere, many men often do. Or, he may possess it in a social sense, and look up at men whom fortune has set in higher social place than himself; and many persons, — even where lovers of equality and fraternity forbid them, — a little shamefacedly, perhaps, often continue to enjoy the contemplation of creatures placed higher than themselves. There may be an element of snobbery in this, but the trait itself does not fall within Thackeray's definition of a mean admiration of mean things; it is a consequence of man's love of the picturesque, of the unfamiliar, of the out-of-reach.

The doings of society, in the narrow sense of the word, consist in dinner parties, balls, *conversazioni*, musicales, teas, frequentations of race tracks and regattas, and other more or less interesting occasions and pretexts for meeting. This social intercourse is accompanied by coaches and handsome motor cars, by awnings and lighted windows, by strains of music, by jewelry and beautiful clothes, by top hats and befurred greatcoats, and all the paraphernalia of property and privilege. Now, politicians apart, this splendor the common man, and especially the common woman, do not grudge; on the contrary, they enjoy it — it is like peeking over the wall into a sophisticated Garden of Eden, it is a free attendance at a theatre, it is a novel shouted aloud. If you are indiscreet, not delicately-minded, and glance at what the women in a suburban train are reading after a day's shopping in New York, you will find that they are reading the news in the social columns, or an account of whatever more dramatic events may have put Mr. A, the well-known frequenter of clubs, or Mrs. X, one of our social leaders, on the front page. There are scores of names to be found in the *New York Social Register* that are more interesting to their fellow citizens than those of all the great lawyers, surgeons, scholars, writers, and artists in the whole nation. This looking up to a freer, gayer, ampler life is by no means to be frowned upon, it is the first rung of the ladder of admiration; other rungs may lead to literature, to poetry, to music, to heroism, to worship, to those celestial contemplations that Diotima sets forth in her golden words, that "the true order of going is to begin from the beauties of the earth and mount upwards . . . from fair forms to fair practices, and from fair practices to fair notions, until from fair notions we arrive at the notion of absolute beauty."

I should say, therefore, that this admiration of

a freer, gayer, ampler life is a good thing — it is like an invalid looking out of a hospital window upon a bustling street. The life of these suburban citizens would be duller, drabber, more disconsolate without it; and I think that in spite of any shamefaced unwillingness to acknowledge the pleasure of it, in spite of the sneers of socialists and humanitarians, this admiration has acted, in its little way, to hinder the total abolition of the Guild of Gentlemen, and has been a pleasant diversion to the lookers-up.

PART THREE

The forces of destruction

XXI

SCIENCE

MY essay so far has attempted to describe
the qualities that marked the Guild of
Gentlemen, according to abstract or academic principles, and secondly as, from time to time, they
have been reported by history. In so doing, this
question presented itself: Did the Guild of Gentlemen have a value to its members great enough to
repay them for the cost of acquiring and maintain-
ing such of the qualities enumerated as are due to
education, discipline, and effort? This question,
it seems to me, has been answered in the affirma-
tive by the persistence of the type through nearly
three thousand years in our Western World. But
a second question followed the first. Did the
Guild have such a value to society at large as to
repay society for the cost of privileges granted
by it to the Guild? This question has now been
answered by democracy in the negative, and that
negative answer is my excuse for this essay. The
motives that induced democracy to reject the

institution seem to me of quite diverse origin, and of very different weight, but such as they are I will present them, not in the order of their importance, but according to convenience and a random habit of mind.

Science prepared the ground for this rejection of traditional values. Her progress during the last half of the nineteenth century, and in the beginning of this, has been one triumphant march; not since Napoleon conducted the campaigns of Ulm and Austerlitz, of Auerstädt, Jena, and Eylau, has our Western World beheld such a series of victories. And the past victories of science are but preparations for future victories. Fifty or sixty years ago, physics was reckoned as one science, chemistry was reckoned as one science; now they are divided and subdivided, and each of the derivative sciences is more wide-embracing than its original then was; and so of a dozen other subjects. Science discourses on what is in the heavens above and the earth beneath, on the habits of the stars and the customs of electrons; it binds the sweet influences of the Pleiades and looses the bands of Orion; it runs its outstretched fingers over the vague convexity that shuts in the farthest reaches of the universe; it delves into nature's secrets, and tells us what has happened and what will happen. Such magical success dominates the human imagination. Science has eclipsed her old competitors — religion and the humanities; she is the cynosure of all eyes; she seems to hold the destinies of humanity in her hand, and sits, without rival, on the intellectual throne.

All the world is shouting that science is modern and looks toward the future, and that religion and the humanities are old and look toward the past; all the world clamors that science, which once was impeded and hindered by religion, has broken religion's bands as Samson broke the green withes, that she has ousted the humanities from the front seats in colleges and schools, and that she has shaken tradition to the foundation. And, with the decline and fall of tradition, all institutions that depend on tradition must decline and fall, too, and one of these institutions is the Guild of Gentlemen.

There is no more talk of the conflict between religion and science; the Church of Rome, with blindfold eyes, goes on its stately way; the Protestant churches are metamorphosing themselves into humanitarian societies, striving to soften and sweeten the common lot, to render it possible for the laboring class to produce all the babies it likes and to employ its leisure agreeably.

Humanists fight gallantly; they contend that man is a creature apart, endowed with will and intellect, and has a law of his own, quite different from the laws that rule in laboratories; but nobody pays much attention to them. Science does not turn her head; her position is so secure that she recks not that the Tree of Knowledge is the Tree of the Knowledge of Good and Evil, and proceeds upon her way, following the gleam of intellectual curiosity, regardless of what consequences may come to human society. Her discoveries have profoundly affected all our moral, mental, and material interests; she has changed the whole organization of society. It was inevitable that all former human values should be shaken, if not wholly overthrown; intellectual curiosity, attended by multitudinous creature comforts, makes such matters as manners, style, taste, modesty, love of privacy, look pale and lustreless. The scientific faculty has displaced the Guild of Gentlemen in the good thoughts of the world.

In short, science has made the way ready for those rearrangements of society that we have seen, and are seeing, take place.

XXII

DEMOCRACY

SCIENCE, by its attention to practical matters, lifted democracy into the saddle, amid the cheers of the humanitarians. And now I proceed to touch upon the consequences to the Guild of Gentlemen. Science, I repeat, did not concern herself primarily with the Guild, for science has nothing to do with human values — she concentrates her attention on phenomena and their interrelations. She codifies what she calls natural laws, and incidentally, while she is pursuing her investigations, she inevitably, all unconsciously, gives a list to social institutions; her acts are essentially democratic, essentially communistic, for whatever she discovers she offers to all for the benefit of all, and so gave democracy the power to get rid of the Guild of Gentlemen.

I am not scholarly enough to say whether democracy was primarily a factor in the dogma of equality, or the dogma of equality a factor in the rise of democracy. The two are closely linked together whether for good or ill, and presumably came to us hand in hand. Under the government of a king, or of an oligarchy, there must have been discontent among the masses, or among influential groups, who deemed that they had grievances; and as against a superior the dogma of equality is an excellent weapon — it is emotional, irrational, and simple.

Apart from the practical use of the dogma as a weapon against a superior class, some philosophers, in their wandering speculations, seem to have hit upon the idea that men were actually born equal. I am told that Locke said men are "by nature free, equal, and independent." Other philosophers and men of liberal thought, illumined or blinded by fraternal emotions, and realizing the sentimental value of the dogma, took it up, and made it the fashion; ambitious men found it an admirable tool for their purposes, and demagogues scattered it as the wind scatters thistledown. "We hold these truths to be self-evident, that all men are created equal." Nothing, perhaps, shows better the working of fashion than the success of this dogma. Fashion is mimicry, and mimicry is the most valuable of the traits we have inherited from our monkey-like ancestors. Mimicry effects an immense economy of effort, and enables a dozen or a hundred to act quickly together in moments of hazard, without stopping to think. It can be carried too far, as with sheep; but without the instinct of imitation culture, civilization, humanity itself, would be impossible. The infant imitates, the child imitates, the adolescent imitates, women imitate, the proletariat imitates; and a fashion, whether for infants, children, adolescents, women, or the proletariat, such as speaking English, drinking orange juice, tying cravats, wearing earrings, or the "self-evident" truth of equality, spreads like wildfire. During the nineteenth century in America, this dogma of human equality was accepted like the multiplication table — taught in schools, asserted in colleges, preached in churches, and shouted from the hustings.

Mr. Aldous Huxley says: "In the case of the theory of democracy the original assumptions are these: that reason is the same and entire in all men, and that all men are naturally equal. To these assumptions are attached several corollaries: that men are naturally good as well as naturally reasonable; that they are the product of their environment; and that they are indefinitely educable." But the fundamental assumption was that of equality, and this assumption, crystallized into dogma, went to work with a vengeance. It established political democracy, it is striving lustily for economic equality, and it has gone far toward social equality — at least it has got so far as to measure social values in terms of money, and therefore, when economic equality shall have been achieved, complete social equality will come. Of these three departments of equality, — political, economic, and social, — the economic, no doubt, is the primary, and that department is rapidly moving on. Economic equality is said to have been established in Russia; it is making progress in England.

Let me borrow a passage quoted by Dean Inge in his *England:* "In all the things that matter there has been an increasing approximation, not separation, of class conditions. There has been a leveling up at one end, and a leveling down at the other. It stares one in the face in visible matters of the first importance — houses, clothes, and locomotion. No one to-day dreams of building a Blenheim, a Chatsworth, or Castle Howard; and no one builds such cottages for laborers as represented the other end of the scale when the palaces were reared. As for clothes, it is no longer possible, as it used to be, to distinguish classes by clothes, masculine or feminine. In the happy days before the arrival of modern capitalism only the rich could travel at all; everyone else was limited to walking. Now all use the same conveyances; the only

appreciable difference between the first and third
class on the railways is the relative amount of
space, and if capitalists dash about the road in
their own cars the proletariat do the same in
char-à-bancs. To-day the poorest emigrants cross
the Atlantic with all the speed and security com-
manded by the rich, whose margin of superiority, ease, and luxury is constantly diminishing." [1]
One needs but read the statistics of motor cars
to know that this process of material equalization
is, in some respects, going on as fast in America
as in England, or faster.

If all this be so, and it seems to be so, how
could it be that the Guild of Gentlemen should
maintain itself; how, with this rage for equality,
shall privilege hold a plea? For the Guild was
the product of all the inequalities and superiorities
that are detestable to the patriotic American man,
and in saying this I do not mean to attribute any
vulgar meanness or envy to this attitude, for the
American, bred upon the Declaration of Independence, holds that these inequalities and superiorities, being contrary to nature, are mere pretense,
affectation, putting on airs, tinsel, sham, frippery.
The action of the many against this privileged
Guild has been all the stronger because the true
democrat is superbly self-righteous, and believes

[1] Quoted from *The Socialist Movement*, by A. Shadwell.

that another man's privilege is a personal injustice to him.

First of all, the gentleman's political prerogatives were swept away. You may trace the process, for example, in the gradual decline in importance of the House of Lords; and a general decline in the political influence of the aristocratic class in England, France, and America has proceeded *pari passu*. Bagehot describes certain aspects of the operation of a democratic constitution in this regard: —

If the acquisition of power is left to the unconscious working of the natural influences of society, the rich and the cultivated will certainly acquire it; they obtain it insensibly, gradually, and without the poorer orders knowing that they are obtaining it; but the result is different when, by the operation of a purely democratic constitution, the selection of rulers is submitted to the direct vote of the populace. The lower orders are then told that they are perfectly able to judge; demagogues assert it to them without ceasing; the constitution itself is appealed to as an incontrovertible witness to the fact — as it has placed the supreme power in the hands of the lower and more numerous classes, it would be contravening it to suppose that the real superiority was in the higher and fewer. Moreover, when men are expressly asked to acknowledge their superiors, they are by no means always inclined to do so; they do not object to yield a mute observance, but they refuse a definite act of homage; they will obey, but they will not *say* that they will obey. In consequence, history teaches that under a democratic government, those who speak the feelings of the majority themselves have a greater chance of being chosen to rule than any of the higher orders, who under another form of government would be admitted to be the better judges. The natural effect of such a government is to mislead the poor.

We have no room to notice the specific evils which would accrue from the adoption of an unmixedly democratic constitution. One, however, which has not been quite appreciated follows naturally from the remarks we have made: there is a risk of vulgarizing the whole tone, method, and conduct of public business. We see how completely this has been done in America. . . . Nor must we imagine that this vulgarity of tone is a mere external expression, not affecting the substance of what is thought or interfering with the policy of the nation: no defect really eats away so soon the political ability of a nation. A vulgar tone of discussion disgusts cultivated minds with the subject of politics; they will not apply themselves to master a topic which, besides its natural difficulties, is encumbered with disgusting phrases, low arguments, and the undisguised language of coarse selfishness. . . . The inevitable consequence of vulgarizing our Parliament would be the deterioration of public opinion, not only in its more refined elements, but in all the tangible benefits we derive from the application to politics of thoroughly cultivated minds.

IN PRAISE OF GENTLEMEN

Bagehot dreads vulgarity, but he does injustice to democracy if he imagines that democracy has any such fears; for democracy is as bold as a lion in confronting vulgarity, absolutely without fear, for indeed it sees in vulgarity only the friendly and familiar. But he is quite right to expect the masses, the *vulgus*, to value their own standards and to act upon their own standards. Cicero said, *"Non est consilium in vulgo, non ratio, non discrimen, non diligentia,"* [1] for Cicero was not only a deep student of men and affairs, but also an aristocrat, and he held a mean opinion of the judgment and acts of the common people: *"Non enim comitiis judicat semper populus, sed movetur plerumque gratia; cedit precibus; facit eos, a quibus est maxime ambitus: denique, si judicat, non dilectu aliquo aut sapientia ducitur ad judicandum, sed impetu nonnumquam et quadam etiam temeritate."* [2] Cicero thought that the people had not reason, or judgment; that they voted from favor, from emotional appeals, from demagogic solicitations — in short, that the *vulgus* was vulgar. That was two thousand years ago,

---

[1] "The common people are not capable of reflection or reason, or discernment."

[2] "In elections the people do not decide right; they are moved by favor, they yield to prayers, they elect those who have most courted them; and, indeed, in their decision they act indiscriminately and foolishly, often impetuously and rashly."

but human nature remains very much as it was.

But I am not concerned here as much with democracy's pushing the gentleman away from his ancient place in the forefront of politics as with democracy's rejection of a gentleman's standards in other matters. That point I will leave for another chapter.

XXIII

BUSINESS

ANOTHER most potent solvent of the old order is business. How remote the economic
structure of the eighteenth century looks. Quiet
as cows in a Constable landscape. Business is the
child of machinery, the grandchild of science; as
one might say Gargantua, son of Grandgousier,
and so on. Science made the tools, and tools
made business. In America, more than elsewhere, there was elbowroom to use the tools.
Prairies, mountains, rivers, seas, opened their arms,
and business proved itself a jolly, thriving wooer.
Business dangled on high a protean prize, and
each man saw in it what he longed for most. The
gambler heard the rattle of the dice, and the
clatter of Fortune's wheel. The romantic saw
rosy gleams flushing the clouds, saw high emprise
like a great ice mountain, scalable, if at all, by
the skin of his teeth, and listened to the sweet
croonings of danger. The avaricious man beheld
bags of gold high piled in safe-deposit vaults; the

glutton smelt the fumes of Haroun-al-Raschid's kitchens; the lecher caught sight of feminine forms fresh from the salt sea foam; the socially-minded fingered the jingling keys that unlock aristocratic doors and bedizened clubrooms; those born in hardship lay on imaginary beds of luxury; and the ambitious man held his shoulders back and his head erect to carry more easily the heavy burden of power.

Up to the Great War business uncurtained its window fronts so that every passer-by, in rags or top hat, might see the Genii of the Ring and of the Lamp ready to work for such as nature had endowed with the right mental formula. Over the whole gamut of life, from lust of bread to lust of power, business shimmered and shone as the giver of all good gifts. The man of reason delighted in the nice adjustments and prophetic vision necessary to success; the artistic man was enamored of the harmony in the processes and of the beauty of happy combinations of forces.

Inevitably business captured the imaginations of the young; and all the youth of America was on fire for material success. As a consequence, those interested in the arts went to Europe, those that cared for literature withdrew from the heady current of national life.

The anti-Guild-of-Gentlemen influence of business in America was aggravated by a special circumstance, known to our historians as the Frontier. Along the western boundary line of that accumulation of usages and customs commonly called our civilization, bands of pioneers cleared forests, massacred Indians, ploughed fields, pastured cattle, in all the freedom of people ignorant of law and indisposed to self-restraint; conscious of an heroic element in their lives, they ignored other human values, and practised themselves, and handed on to the crowds following at their heels, a contempt of law, of covenants, of manners and other usages that people enervated by tradition had been wont to observe. This heritage from the Frontier inoculated business with its spirit of enterprise, independence, heroic endeavor, and indifference to the usages and customs talked about in books on ethics. And there followed what persons out of sympathy with this economic development call the piracy of big business.

Let me quote Lowes Dickinson's description of the American man of business, as he saw him: "Describe the average Western man and you describe the American; from east to west, from north to south, everywhere and always the same — masterful, aggressive, unscrupulous, egotistic, and at once good-natured and brutal, kind if you do not cross him, ruthless if you do, greedy, ambitious, self-reliant, active for the sake of activity, intelligent and unintellectual, quick-witted and crass, contemptuous of ideas but amorous of devices, valuing nothing but success, recognizing nothing but the actual. . . . The impression America makes upon me is that the windows are blocked up."

I mention these phenomena, without praise or blame, merely to explain how impossible it became for the Guild of Gentlemen, with its love of manners, of style, of taste, of privacy, of decency, of the humanities, to continue to be a social force under such circumstances.

XXIV

SPECIALIZATION

ANOTHER, but lesser, enemy of the Guild of Gentlemen is our modern device of specialization. This is a hybrid product of increased population and science; there are a great many more things to be done than there were a hundred years ago, and a great many more people to do them. Actual existing human wants are multitudinous, and potential wants, to be discovered as science shall more and more discover the means of satisfying them, will come to birth, turn into greedy appetites, and be more numerous still. The number of occupations keeps pace with the growth of wants, and each occupation demands labor of special kind, laborers of special aptitudes, and consequently workingmen are more and more divided and subdivided into groups, each group more and more concentrated upon its own task, and more and more ignorant of other occupations, even where such other occupations are necessary in the construction of a whole upon which all are at work.

SPECIALIZATION

Take a department store, for an example in miniature. On entering, you are greeted by a doorkeeper, whose business it is to unravel the perplexities of local geography to you. Next you meet the warder of the elevators, also a friend to the needy: "Beaded goods, madam? Third floor left." "Toys, fifth floor right." "Overshoes, sir, basement, and inquire there." The elevator boy: "First floor! Trimmings, crockery, drugs, bath towels!" "Second floor! Flowerpots, cheeses!" And so on. You are met on your particular floor by a polite floorwalker: "This way, sir, last counter but one, on your left." One young woman is in charge of handkerchiefs, another of markings in silk, a third of men's gloves, a fourth of fleece-lined gloves, and so on and so on. It is a mercantile education to walk the mile or two of corridors between counters. There are hundreds of salesfolk, each with his or her own task, and, except for the floorwalkers, who are only peripatetic signposts, all are ignorant of the next salesman's goods. Multiply this by ten thousand or a hundred thousand, and you have but a fraction of the various employments of men in our Western World. The professions are divided and subdivided. Physicians specialize; lawyers, merchants, thieves, all and each, have their particular piece of work.

IN PRAISE OF GENTLEMEN

The sum of knowledge is enormous, and putting it piece by piece to the satisfaction of human wants more and more obliges each man to limit himself to the bit of knowledge necessary for his task. This is inevitable, and, if blameworthy, no individual is to be blamed; if praiseworthy, no individual is to be praised. And in like manner as these material occupations have been separated and each put into confinement, so it has been, in a measure, with the notes, or such of them as survive, that used to mark a gentleman; you will find one set of men employed in naval and military service, apart by themselves; another set engaged in political life off by themselves; men of fashion by themselves; men who value privacy by themselves; lovers of the humanities by themselves. The centrifugal forces of society, while leveling and equalizing, have broken up the old fraternity in which were united men of many interests, all of whom shared the qualities common to gentlemen, although each one, according to his tastes or the circumstances of his life, cultivated one occupation more than any other.

Specialization has done away with the dilettante. And this doing away with the dilettante is highly gratifying to democrats, humanitarians, realists, men of science, and all who approve and enjoy the social forces that dominate our modern world. It is not for me to venture to suggest that they are not in the right, but as the dilettante was closely connected under the old régime with the gentleman, and is now sharing the same fate, I feel it not irrelevant to say a few words in his favor, if such can be found without straining the duties of an advocate. The specialist is grave and serious, and usually wears spectacles; he is concerned with the future of humanity, for the particular thing he does appears to him an essential element in that future. He can proudly deny that he ever was, in any respect, the doubter or the doubt; he is the handiwork of belief. Whatever his occupation or interest, whether he be at work upon a pin, a poisonous gas, a criticism of the quantum theory, the reconciliation of capital and labor, a bar of music or a *vers libre*, he is a believer. To him has been denied *l'art de sourire de son œuvre*. The inanimate forces of nature all take themselves seriously; and the specialist, whether in a bank or helping grind a telescope lens, feels that his place is among them, that he, too, is part of our energetic cosmos, and, like his fellow forces, should go about with a grave aspect.

The dilettante, on the other hand, has a lightsome eye, and affects a feather of the blue; he takes life easily and, thanks to his light-mindedness, walks buoyantly over thin crusts where more solid minds break through. He is a great admirer of pleasant things, pleasant places, pleasant people, pleasant occupations, and therefore attaches importance to the exterior of things; and this is one of the traits he has in common with the gentleman. He prefers acquaintance to knowledge, he likes better the surface of the earth than those subterranean tunnels in which the serious-minded burrow. He likes to flit from subject to subject, from interest to interest, to gather nectar as the bees do, and perhaps he sets too high a value upon honey. He prefers skimming to diving, multiplicity to unity, diversion to devotion, the random to the systematic, the hypothesis of coincidence to that of cause and effect. If he must choose between enjoyment and comprehension, he chooses enjoyment. He likes style almost as much as matter, and sets great store by good taste. He had rather read comedy than tragedy, and books about good fellows than subtle psychological analyses concerning characters one would fight shy of in life. He entertains a kindly feeling for jacks-of-all-trades, and likes to watch a blacksmith, a billiard player, a chemist, a prize fighter, a painter, a gardener, a bricklayer, a veterinary, at their several occupations, but never for very long.

SPECIALIZATION

These dilettanti, as I say, are not held in good repute; no more were earthworms before Charles Darwin revealed their uses. The dilettanti take in ideas crudely, turn them over in their minds, peel off obscurities, smooth rugosities, and pass the ideas on, in a form more readily understandable, to other dilettanti, who continue the process of peeling and smoothing, and finally hand on to the mass of the less educated, not the original ideas, but ideas, smeared with the commonplace and deformed by ready intelligibility, which nevertheless possess a quality that the original ideas did not have, the quality of awakening general curiosity. And some qualities, which I specified as notes of the gentleman, — style, taste, and good manners, — the dilettante treats with great seriousness. In these matters, if not a profound critic, he is a stimulating virtuoso, if only by putting forth wrong explanations of theories concerning works of art, or national policies, or new biological hypotheses, and rousing the many to thinking at all about such things.

The dilettante, like an accomplished host, kept the Guild of Gentlemen together; he brought the whole company into mutual relations, into common sympathies and a common understanding; he reformulated their ideals and renovated their traditions. He maintained this consciousness of unity among them by a gay, sprightly insistence upon the transitoriness of things, and on the essential value of transitoriness to the human soul; by skepticism as to the knowability of the future, and a merry aloofness from every current philosophy; by preaching and teaching the value of sport, of the heroic, and of the useless; and by his debonair refusal to agree that the essence of existence is the grave matter that sad-eyed men declare it to be.

Specialization has, as we say, put the dilettante out of business; it loosed the cord that held the Guild of Gentlemen together, and so helped render it defenseless before the assaults of triumphant democracy.

XXV

LESSER DISAPPROBATIONS

I REPEAT, the old-fashioned notes that distinguished members of the Guild of Gentlemen — manners, style, modesty, taste, liking for privacy, making much of the humanities — are not in the good graces of democracy. Science opened the way, for science does not care for any of these qualities, any more than she cares for religion, or beauty, or the welfare of mankind, or human happiness; those things are not her affair. She has but one interest, the increase of knowledge. But despite the irrelevancy of what science thinks of these matters, her prestige is so immense that her indifference to them is always an argument ready to hand for the lovers of equality, and a justification for turning up their noses at them as matters of no moment. Democracy is, perhaps, rather indifferent than hostile to the traits in question, for, like science, democracy has other interests, other duties, as she would express it — she must busy

herself with the elementary wants of the masses,
with housing, with feeding, with providing work,
with shortening hours of labor and increasing pay,
and providing amusement. She regards manners
as Harry Hotspur did the fop: —

> Came there a certain lord, neat, and trimly dressed,
> Fresh as a bridegroom . . .
> He was perfumed like a milliner,
> And 'twixt his finger and his thumb he held
> A pouncet-box.

To democracy, manners are a pouncet box;
she would merely ridicule them if all were well
with the masses, but when she sees hunger, disease,
want, misery, vice, despair, she becomes savage
and unreasonable; she denounces the care of manners as so much time and attention stolen from
pity and help. I read in M. Emile Faguet: "The
question is often asked why politeness is ebbing
away day by day, and everybody laughs and answers, 'Because of Democracy.' . . . Politeness
is a mark of respect, of subservience. Now, that
is not democratic, because democracy does not acknowledge any superiority, and so does not feel
respect, nor permit any expression of personal
subservience. Respect means to put oneself lower
than someone else; politeness towards an equal
is the affectation of regarding him as a superior.

This is wholly contrary to the democratic spirit. There is no superiority of any kind."

And, more than this, democracy is the expression of the wishes, the appetites, the taste of the many, and naturally she is indifferent to the wishes, the appetites and tastes, of the few; she prefers her own ways, as an Englishman prefers his ways to a Frenchman's, or as an American prefers his ways to those of a Japanese. It is hard to strike a balance between the wants of the many and the tastes of the few; the shibboleth of the greatest good to the greatest number, preached by the utilitarians, is satisfactory to the greatest number but not to the few. Quality against quantity is a matter on which people differ. The aristocrat holds for quality, the democrat for quantity, and as, under a democracy, the many are the judges, the advocates of quantity have it. This brings us to another form of the old question, Is civilization worth while, is the philosopher better off than the earthworm? The Guild of Gentlemen maintained that manners added a value to life; that they made human intercourse pleasanter; that, like other arts, they enriched human experience; that the birth, growth, and development of all the arts are proofs of their value; that the persistence of the minority in prizing them, in spite of the indifference or antagonism of the majority, shows that they really are essential to the human soul.

There are, of course, individuals who, without property, training, or privilege, have good manners. Emerson has much to say about nature's gentlemen. Such cases are exceptional. Manners, like other customs, are taught; fine manners are an art; they consist in a number of conventions: how to stand, how to sit; how to address the old, the middle-aged, the young; how to handle knife and fork; how to begin a conversation with a shy young lady; how to enter a drawing-room; how to dress; how, before looking, to hand the dictionary to the other person when there is a disagreement concerning the spelling of a word. Civility, in the eyes of those who have never experienced it, is a matter of indifference, like a watch to a Hottentot, or a Bible to a man that cannot read, but, once become familiar, it is like salt — without it human intercourse loses a great part of the flavor. The democrat says, "I live according to Nature, who made men free, equal, and independent." But how can we be sure that we should trust Nature in this matter? La Rochefoucauld says: *"La plupart des jeunes gens croient être naturels lorsqu'ils ne sont que mal polis et grossiers"* — most young men think that they are behaving naturally when they are really uncivil and rude.

LESSER DISAPPROBATIONS

Style is but a specialization of manners in various fields, and is displeasing to democracy for the same reasons; it appears foppish, an assumption of superiority, a diversion of attention from the primary human interests to the minutiæ of preciosity. Such an estimate is inevitable if we accept the dogma of equality and the common definition, *Le style, c'est l'homme;* democracy believes that equality does or should exist among all men, and that therefore style should be alike for all — natural motions of the body, putting one's feet on the mantelpiece, unselected words proceeding from untrained throats, the vocabulary of the American reporter, the conversation of the smoking car, the civility of a taxi driver. Style, perhaps, is as conspicuous in the art of singing as anywhere; it means training, trills, practice, restraint, effort, as well as voice and ear; but the principle of equality demands the mere opening of the mouth and emission of sound. Nothing troubles the democratic conscience so much as the exceptional; and style implies rampant individualism. Once upon a time, old father antic Tradition propounded certain opinions concerning style in literature: the best for prophecy is Isaiah's; for elegance, sweetness, and force, Cardinal Newman's; for biography, Boswell's; for plain dogmatic narration, Macaulay's; for a sermon, Jeremy

Taylor's; for art concealing art, *The Vicar of Wakefield*, and so on. It was thought that in every kind of literature there is a style best suited to the subject; but style has been granted to very few, wholly denied to most, and has no part or portion in any aspect of the self-evident truth of equality. Democracy, as you may see in almost every American newspaper and journal, rejects it as a badge of a privileged class.

It is the same with taste. The classical theory was that taste, whether in matters of art or in ethical questions, is the trained judgment of a man of peculiar sensitiveness and education, or rather the collective judgment of men of peculiar sensitiveness and education. Aristotle made a clear distinction between the cultivated audience and the uncultivated audience: one derived pleasure from one sort of performance, the other from another. The distinction was one of taste. As the uncultivated majority is immensely larger than the cultivated minority, and the majority believes in equality, the standard of the majority becomes orthodox, and any divergence from that is discountenanced as part of the frippery of aristocratic theories.

As for modesty, the rights of the public are so dominating and domineering that any person who catches its attention is deemed public property by

right of democratical eminent domain, and his life
becomes as unveiled as a book by one of our physi-
ological novelists; he lives in a glass house, and
the natural rights of other men include the right
to stare at him. Privacy is the very finest brand
of caviar to the general; it is Sanskrit to them;
they have the right to see, to inspect, to photo-
graph, to intrude wherever curiosity may lead
them. The man who would be alone, who does
not care to rub elbows with the crowd, who finds
the mass of his fellow men unsympathetic and
unattractive, is a monster. How the whirligig of
time has brought its revenges! How distasteful
it is for us to read of Coriolanus addressing his
fellow citizens: —

You common cry of curs . . . whose loves I prize
As the dead carcasses of unburied men
That do corrupt my air!

or to hear the Tribune Marullus say: —

You blocks, you stones, you worse than senseless things!

whereas now our public men are always very polite to their fellow citizens and lard their speeches
with praises of the industry, intelligence, good
heart, sound sense, ungullibility, and other such
qualities that we, the masses, happily believe we
possess. If we, the masses, are always right in

[179]

our collective judgments, we must be right to condemn those guilty of the social fault of loving privacy.

The humanities fare no better. Science here as elsewhere prepared the way; she displaced religion, she displaced the humanities. Scholars in vain contended that man as man has his own territory; that he is not to be dismissed as an aggregate of forces held together by some wayward whim of cohesion, as a quantity of neighborly atoms crowded into an ape-like mould; that he is *sui generis;* that his history is of primary importance to himself, and has never been told so vividly, so concisely, or so beautifully, as in Greek and Latin literature. Their arguments were of no avail. Chemists, physicists, biologists, have crowded professors and teachers of Greek and Latin out of college lecture halls and out of schoolrooms; and upon library shelves, public or private, in the place of Homer, Sophocles, Plato, Thucydides, Horace, Vergil, Cicero, and such, stand books by Einstein, Eddington, Jeans, Haldane, and other eminent men of science. Democracy approves the change: she can understand the practical advantages of applied science, of mass production, of facilities of locomotion, of the pleasures of the radio and the cinema, of cheaper food and less work, and she turns indignantly upon the humanists and asks what they have done for the masses: Will they give Greek poetry to factory hands? Will they give Latin prose to navvies, longshoremen, miners, stokers? The humanist can only urge that the man "who has assimilated the riches of tradition and is harmoniously developed and wise in himself" is of necessity beneficial to his fellow men, and so back to the old argument that an exceptional cultivated class is of advantage to the community.

In short, the lover of equality rejects all the inequalities that he can, and the humanitarian is forced by the very objects of his sympathy to concentrate his attention upon physical needs.

XXVI

HUMANITARIANISM

THE cult of the Genus Homo derives from altruism, and altruism is, as I believe, a far too sweeping deduction from the history of mankind. A man is a social animal, I admit; and more than that, he is the product of the society in which he is born. He receives his words, his usages, his habits of eating, dressing, talking, thinking, from the people about him. The baby is dependent upon its mother, the child upon its nurse, the boy upon his masters, the youth upon his father, and everybody gets his education from all the people with whom he comes into contact. The individual receives from society almost everything. Moralists, therefore, — and it is amazing how certain men, even certain classes of men, like to lay down dogmas in morals, — assert that it is a man's duty to do everything possible for society, give labor, time, thought, affection, even his life, to his fellow men, grouped into a family, a city, a tribe, a nation, or wherever found. There is no such duty to animals in general, merely to the human species. And man does give as much as he receives; he is obliged to. The shoemaker will not part with his shoes unless he is paid, and paid the full equivalent, and so it is for whatever a man gets; he pays back in dollars, in thanks, in affection, by barter, by exchange. But this is not altruism; altruism means that a man shall give something for nothing.

This social system has been so necessary for man that humanitarians assume, with charming enthusiasm, that a man should do everything for society, and that society should do everything for man. The theory passes rapidly from the realm of reason to that of emotion; it is so much pleasanter and more comfortable to float down on the current of emotion than to climb the steep hill of reason. Even philosophers become humanitarian. And the general cry is that altruism is virtue. And yet nothing is simpler than to perceive that this is an emotional fallacy. An altruist is one who does things for another person; an egotist is one who does things for himself. In Dreamland Avenue, a suburb of Utopia, live James and John, two altruists, who live according to their creed. The day begins badly, for they cannot wake each other up; but they do the best they can, for one wakes the other in turn, day by day. Once they

are up, however, altruism is steadily practised.
No Unitarian humanitarian could do better. John
washes James and brushes James's teeth. James
washes John and brushes John's teeth. After the
bath they dry one another. At breakfast James
feeds John his egg, John does the same for James.
They simultaneously pour coffee into each other's
mouth. This required much practice, and it was
necessary to administer the coffee by spoonfuls —
One! two! three! open! swallow! — before they
even attempted pouring from the cup directly
down each other's throat. Putting on, each upon
the other, coat, hat, rubbers, and gloves was a
gratifying ceremony. Unfortunately each had to
walk on his own legs to the train. Once down-
town, each did the other's job — and so on, each
feeding the other at lunch and at dinner, and putting the other to bed. James and John are altruists. Opposite them live two fellows, Andrew
and Peter, and each one does the various activities
I have enumerated for himself; they are egotists.

From this I infer that although man is a social
animal, and is the product of society, there comes
a point at which altruism should stop and a man
should think for himself and act for himself. If
moralists think that egotism means self-indulgence,
it need not. The task of the egotist — if he cares
for duty, for stoicism, for effort, and ideal ends, as

some do — is not easy. He may develop his body so that it shall be adequate for all sorts of labor, exercising at hard and dangerous games, — a task rarely performed by altruists, although they often build gymnasiums for others, — eating for health and not for pleasure, early to bed and early to rise. He may develop his mind by hard thinking, laboring over mathematics, philosophy, chemical formulæ, physical hypotheses, or over Lucretius and Thucydides. He may observe all the rules of Fortitudo, Temperantia, Justitia, and Prudentia, and tread, never overstepping, the golden mean.

As you see, the Guild of Gentlemen have always inclined to the doctrines of the egotist; they have striven after the virtues of the egotist, and they have fallen into the faults of the egotist — arrogance, self-indulgence, hardness of heart. The altruists, humanitarians, are products of the herd instinct, and love the herd; and the herd, with its passion for sameness, is steadily striving to establish universal conformity, and abolish all nonconformist bodies, and so it has been one of the active factors in the suppression of the Guild of Gentlemen.

XXVII

SUCCESS

THERE is a particular element in these forces of destruction, or reformation, that must not be passed over unnoticed. I refer to the popular admiration of what is called success. Under the old régime success was limited in kind; that is to say, there was success in war, in deeds of high enterprise, in piety, in poetry, in magnificence; and it was not called success, but renown. And this difference of words indicates a difference of ideas. Renown was not mere achievement of notoriety. Achilles, Pericles, Marcus Aurelius, Saint Francis of Assisi, the starry Galileo, Christopher Columbus, Milton, and so on, achieved renown. For instance, read Milton's lines: —

> But chief
> Thee Sion and the flowrie Brooks beneath
> That wash thy hallow'd feet, and warbling flow,
> Nightly I visit: nor sometimes forget
> Those other two equal'd with me in Fate,

SUCCESS

So were I equal'd with them in *renown*,
Blind Thamyris and blind Mæonides.

It would have been a bold man that should go
to Milton and congratulate him on his *success*.
Renown implied an element of nobility, of mag-
nanimity, of high endeavor, of generous purpose,
united with rare powers of brain or brawn. It
was a word for poetry and epitaphs, not lightly
won, not lightly given.

But if to-day, here in America, a referendum
were to be held, what names would appear on the
popular ballot? The President of the United
States occupies a position apart — by his office of
itself he has gained a permanent name in history;
but of other men, who would receive the encomium
of success from the masses? Would it be the jus-
tices of the Supreme Court, the leaders of the bar
in New York and Chicago, the most skillful surgeons, the most learned physicians, the most profound scientists, the most thoughtful of our writers,
or any of those who in privacy, struggling against
heavy odds, by patience, perseverance, courage,
and high hope, have done what to them seemed
the highest? No; I could pick a list of the most
notable in the eyes of the masses, if it were not
invidious. It would surely include some ball
player, some cinema star, some editor whose jour-

[187]

nal had reached the circulation of a million, or
two or three, a magnate in some branch of industry, and every one would be measured by a measure largely based upon money. No one, or hardly
anyone, — for it is long since Saint Francis of
Assisi celebrated his espousals with Lady Poverty
and

Poscia di dì in dì l'amò più forte, —

runs after Poverty. On the contrary, we all agree
with Quevedo, —

Poderoso caballero es don Dinero, —

and success without money is thought to be a hu-
morous paradox. The second element, necessary
to win popular approval, is novelty — whether
in use of language, of paintbrush, sculptor's chisel,
or what not. The third necessary element is widespread notoriety. Combine these three ingredients, money, novelty, and notoriety, and you have
the common conception of success.

If you were to instance Colonel Lindbergh,
who has achieved renown equal to that of Vasco
da Gama, or Captain Cook, it is doubtful if a popular vote would include him among the very
successful men of to-day; so universal with us is
the idea that money must enter into success. We
are not more loving of money than other peoples,

[188]

but money is so convenient a measure of merit and so readily understood that, under the democratic notion that the opinion of the masses shall decide reputation, success almost necessarily implies money.

Here, again, a notion entertained by democracy hurtles against a notion entertained by the Guild of Gentlemen. For the gentleman (as I have repeatedly said) believes in tradition and likes privacy. In every definition of a gentleman it is necessary to say that he is a man that believes in tradition and likes privacy; and although, and there seems to be inconsistency here, the gentleman stands upon property, and usually inherited property, he refuses to accept wealth in any respect as a measure of success, nor will he accept novelty *per se*, or notoriety in any form, as among the good things of life. Inevitably democracy cries out, "Away with such fellows, away with the Guild of Gentlemen."

And what will be the final result? Let me quote Lecky once again: "Modern democracy is not favorable to the higher forms of intellectual life. Democracy levels down quite as much as it levels up. The belief in the equality of man, the total absence of the spirit of reverence, the apotheosis of the average judgment, the fever and the haste, the advertising and sensational spirit

IN PRAISE OF GENTLEMEN

which American life so abundantly generates, and which the American press so vividly reflects, are all little favorable to the productions of great works of beauty or of thought, of long meditation, of sober taste, of serious, uninterrupted study."

EPILOGUE

WHEN one reflects upon this rising flood of democracy, political, economic, social, and its great sweep towards an equality of human conditions, — similar houses, similar food, the same clothes, the same education, the same manners, the same bath in the sunshine of publicity, the same freedom from the old burdens of Latin and Greek, — one has a sense of bewilderment; for although all the waves and billows that make the flood seem to be going one way, — at least while you look at the main current, or listen to street orators, to philanthropists, communists, Unitarian clergymen, and such other lovers of their kind, — yet, nevertheless, if you dive a little below the surface, if you stop your ears to those eloquent voices, you become aware of lesser currents that run athwart or directly counter to the main flood. I do not refer to Fascism, to those countries which, disappointed by political democracy, have turned to autocracy, but to those social currents at work everywhere about us in industrial life, both here and in Europe. I mean the permanent oligarchic or aristocratic element in human society.

In the New England town meeting, which we have all been taught to honor, there was pure democracy, women apart, for each man had a vote; and so, too, in ancient Greek cities; and nowadays political democracy tries to retain this purity by the referendum, by pledging representatives to vote according to the instructions of their constituents, and so on, but such expedients can only be of limited application and of doubtful expediency. In times of stress, as in the Great War, it has always been necessary to set up a virtual autocracy, and now in our economic difficulties the country has conferred autocratic powers on the President. But it is not political autocracies such as these that I have in mind.

In every group of men the ablest take control of the group's business, partly because the others are apathetic, or lazy, or because they are sensible and wish the business of the group to be well conducted. This is obvious in all economic matters; the able few become a directing oligarchy; they become the brain of the body; they think, plan, devise, and act. It is the same in trade-unions, it is the same everywhere: a capable minority controls and directs. Wherever practical matters of business are concerned, the rhetorical dogma of human equality is quite forgotten. The oligarchies, as a rule, only exercise their power in their particular corporation, union, convention, or assembly, or whatever it may be, and are not leaders in other departments of life. The oligarchy in control of the oil industry does not dictate fashions in dress; that in control of the textile union does not prescribe rules of manners; the directors of the stockyards do not set up a standard of taste; the leaders of the Brotherhood of Engineers do not concern themselves with the study of Greek and Latin. It is the same story in all human interests: a small group, distinguished by exceptional ability, dominates the whole membership. But all these able oligarchs are disunited; each set attends to its own concerns. The principal achievement of democracy has been, not to prevent oligarchs, or aristocrats, — the best men, — from ruling, but to keep each set separate and apart, so that they no longer constitute a class.

In former times these sets of oligarchs were not separate and apart, they were mingled and blended in one whole. They intermarried; they shared various occupations and pleasures; they specialized much less; they combined their interests much more. The soldier discussed plans of a manor house with the humanist — where dormer windows should be put, or how chimneys should be built in order to draw well; the man of fashion argued questions of taste with the statesman; the bishop disputed over windows, tombs, mosaics, with architect, sculptor, and painter; and all went off together to shoot grouse, or hunt the fox; they walked together, talked together, dined, drank brandy, ale, or coffee together, danced together, went to church together; they created an atmosphere, a school of behavior; they brought their body of beliefs into order and system; they codified their conventions, and established the Guild of Gentlemen.

But now there is no general oligarchy which combines all the functions of the old Guild of Gentlemen; one exercises authority here, one there; they remain separate oligarchies, and there seems no tendency for any universal combination. The reason seems to be that democracy, though it has failed to overcome the unconquerable inequality among men, has been able to crush out all the subsidiary qualities that belonged to the old dominant minority, and held it together, — eupatridæ, patricians, feudal barons, lords, nobles, aristocrats, or whatever name has been given to them, — all those qualities that I enumerated at length in my first part.

There remain vestiges of the old sense of military duty in the rush of young patricians to enlist

in time of war; there are remnants of political
duty in "public spirit," usually manifested by con-
tributions of money to reforming societies, but

> . . . Where gentry, title, wisdom,
> Cannot conclude but by the yea and no
> Of general ignorance,

such public spirit is but fire in straw; and as to the
lesser matters of manners, style, modesty, taste,
privacy, and love of traditional values, they have
gone hopelessly down before the assaults of democracy. The wreckage of these old traditions is
being cleared away, and the brave new world,
neat and fresh, spick and span, full of liberty (tempered by autocracy or anarchy), full of fraternity
(mitigated by suspicion, hatred, and war), and
full of oligarchic control hidden under the mask
of equality, may take its shining way, to the content
of humanitarians and reformers.

And if the Guild of Gentlemen be gone, and
gone forever, let there be soldier's music for their
passage, for in their time they did gallant deeds,
made splendid the pageant of history, and bequeathed to us ennobling memories: —

> Men are we, and must grieve when even the shade
> Of that which once was great is passed away.